# WHO IS IN YOUR PERSONAL BOARDROOM?

## Praise for *Who is in your Personal Boardroom?*

'The Personal Boardroom is a great addition to our narrative around leadership and it has proved to be highly valuable to our members. It is a simple and clear concept for leaders, easily grasped and implemented.'

Liam Black,
Chief Encouragement Officer, The Same Wavelength

'This is a brilliant, simple and intuitive way to set about personal and career development. The Personal Boardroom is a powerful concept that can help us all throughout our working lives, even in this world of accelerating change.'

Matt Brittin,
Vice President, Northern and Central Europe Operations, Google

'Having worked much of my career in complex, global organisations I wish I had read this book years ago. Navigating how decisions are made, resources are allocated and people are promoted is immeasurably easier with the right Personal Boardroom. Since I have started consciously engaging people to help me as Navigators, Unlockers, Sponsors and Influencers, I've seen the huge value this can add. The Personal Boardroom approach is an immensely practical way to help you succeed in any business role, and the more complex your working world, the more valuable it will be.'

Dan Cobley
Former Managing Director, UK and Ireland, Google

'The Personal Boardroom diagnostic really helped me to consider whether I had the right mix and balance in my network to support me in achieving my personal and career goals. It's something I will revisit on a regular basis and I'm already using the concept with others.'

Lynne Connelly,
Head of Talent

'Our connections are everything. Humans by our very nature are social creatures. Our connections enrich our lives and it is through these relationships that in many ways we understand who we truly are and what is really important to us. In this thoughtful book Zella and Amanda encourage us to think about what they elegantly describe as our 'Personal Boardroom'—our current and potential connections and how they may support us in what we want to achieve. Well worth reading!'

Piers Fallowfield-Cooper,
Executive Chairman, Greycon Ltd

Zella King and Amanda Scott have nailed the secret of modern career success: having the right connections and knowing who to ask for help from and how to help others in equal measure. *Who is in your Personal Boardroom?* should become something of a corporate classic.

Julia Hobsbawm,
Honorary Visiting Professor in Networking, Cass Business School,
and founder, Editorial Intelligence

'The Personal Boardroom approach helped with the hardest thing of all: taking hundreds of contacts and connections and finding six great people who are happy to give me honest advice on that most delicate subject—my own future.'

Adrian Keogh,
Global drinks marketer and entrepreneur

'*Who is in your Personal Boardroom?* brings together great insights and useable principles that will grow your personal and professional impact. It's a handbook for our times and I know you'll enjoy reading and implementing every chapter.'

John McGrane
Director, The British Irish Chamber of Commerce

'In this easy-reading guide, Amanda and Zella have captured the essence of strategic networking and created a framework that is arguably essential for career advancement in today's complex corporate organisations. Their step-by-step approach to selecting and building your Personal Boardroom will open your eyes to the people around you and the roles they can play to contribute to your success.'

Teresa Purthill
Vice President, Global Customer Care, Hertz Corporation

'At last, some practical advice on networking! We are genetically endowed with social networking skills—it is part of what makes the human species so effective. We know good networking drives success, but how do we get better at it? Simply trying harder is not the answer. We need a clear goal and a strategy for achieving it. The Personal Boardroom is a simple but powerful framework for doing just that. For anyone looking for a more effective network, this is essential reading.'

John Wells,
Professor of Management Practice, Harvard Business School

# WHO IS IN YOUR PERSONAL BOARDROOM?

## How to choose people, assign roles and have conversations with purpose

By **Zella King** and **Amanda Scott**

# Preface

By Maria O'Donoghue
Vice President, Global Learning and Talent Management
The Hertz Corporation

Like many people, I have always been intuitively aware of the importance of relationships, formal and informal, in getting results. At some level, we are all aware of the importance of doing our groundwork before important meetings, ensuring that key decision-makers are well briefed and, hopefully, bought in. And who doesn't feel more confident when they have an advocate or sponsor in their corner, somebody who supports them in their career ambitions and gives them the advice and guidance they need to be successful?

Mentoring programs go some way towards developing such relationships but there is still considerable scope for organisations to promote and capitalise on the power of networks—internal and external, formal and informal—to enable and accelerate success. For that reason, I invited Zella and Amanda to pilot their work with me and some of my colleagues at Hertz over a six-month period, with the objective of developing a conscious competence in the art and science of identifying, engaging and leveraging the skills and experience of people who would support, guide and challenge us to perform at our best.

We were all in transition. Some of us were joining Hertz from an acquired company; another had received a significant promotion and was relocating to a different geography; another was moving from a divisional role to a global role; and in my case, I was taking on additional responsibility and a bigger team, and wanted to up my game in terms of my leadership and influencing skills.

What attracted me to the Personal Boardroom was that it seemed to offer a structured approach to becoming more aware of and more considered about the people who would be the enablers of success. Like any board of directors, the key role of people in our Personal Boardroom is to ensure our success and prosperity by providing direction, advice and guidance. Each person will bring something different to the table: challenge, expertise, connections, inspiration, *etc.* Previously I would have more than likely sought advice, guidance and sponsorship either from people like me or from people I liked—my family, friends, trusted colleagues. But I came to understand that they may not always be the best people to challenge me, or question my assumptions or present a different point of view.

What I also like about the Personal Boardroom concept is that it gives us a framework as well as practical tools and techniques to reflect and make choices about who we need to be in our Personal Boardrooms, what role we need them to play, and how to have those important discussions to recruit members and bring them on board. The Personal Boardroom methodology is structured and visual, making it easy to see gaps and opportunities in your network.

It is also very practical. With a focus on both your current situation and your future aspirations, it brings a conscious consideration of who is going to be important on your journey. It will help you tap into the wealth of knowledge and expertise you have at your fingertips: those professional connections—either in your present or previous jobs—where you may be able to receive or give support.

Another thing I really like is the emphasis on paying it forward, on considering what we can offer to others. This could be used very powerfully by an organisation to create a culture of give and take, of collaboration, sponsorship, and mutual support, focused not just on individual performance but also on team and organisational success. Taking this a step further, wouldn't it be a wonderful world if everyone was working to help others be successful? Imagine if everyone was clear about what they needed, while at the same time making themselves available to help others?

As part of the Personal Boardroom programme, each of us had frequent coaching calls with Zella or Amanda to review and talk through important relationships and to plan how to engage other people in our Personal Boardrooms as our circumstances changed. This work helped us create, from the get-go, the foundations of strong relationships that would be important for longer term success in our new roles.

The business benefit was that the people involved in the pilot became effective, productive and comfortable in their new roles more quickly. Typically, when people are selected for roles, they are equipped with the technical skills and competence to do their jobs; but ultimately what differentiates a good company from a great company is how people work together. The Personal Boardroom framework provided us with a way to fast-track our success and gave us the tools and the confidence to start building and leveraging relationships for the good of the business.

The Personal Boardroom concept has several applications in leadership, management development, coaching and mentoring. It is a unique way of helping people to assess where they are now, and where they need to be in terms of the critical relationships for success. It also provides a powerful framework for being thoughtful about the science of working with other people. I just wish it had been around thirty years ago when I was beginning my career journey!

Maria O'Donoghue
Vice President, Global Learning and Talent Management
The Hertz Corporation

# Contents

# How to use this book

*You're only as good as who you surround yourself with.*

Peter Sims, author of
True North: Discover your Authentic Leadership[1]

In the West, we live in a society that emphasises standing alone. Stories of success in business and leadership are narrated as heroic journeys of individual achievement against the odds. But curiously, if you tell someone the statement above—*you're only as good as who you surround yourself with*—they will nod wisely. Instinctively, people accept that one of the keys to becoming and remaining effective as a leader is having a support group around you.

So it is surprising how little time people spend thinking about that support group: who should be in it, when to involve people, what help to ask for, and how to ask in a way that isn't needy, and is useful. In our work with hundreds of executives, including some very senior individuals, we continually find that people have never thought in a structured way about who they surround themselves with. Everyone pays lip service to the importance of networks; but few people think carefully about how to select, from all the connections they have, the ideal combination of people that will equip them for success in their career, and as a leader of their business.

*Few people think carefully about how to select the ideal combination of people who can equip them for success.*

Since 2012, we have been using our Personal Boardroom™ diagnostic tool with executives in large organisations and small companies. The tool asks a few simple questions about the small group of people (typically 6–12) who can most help you to succeed.

We have found that the diagnostic tool does a great job of getting people to ask questions they have not thought about before, such as:

*Am I surrounding myself with the right people?*

Some of your relationships are obvious: your boss, your team, senior managers, a mentor or an important investor are all going to have an impact on your success. But what about the rest of the people you know, both professionally and personally? How you invest time with the rest of your network is up to you. It's likely that you spend a lot of time with some people, while others you don't see for years at a time. Along the spectrum that spans from close, trusting relationships to infrequent and distant ones, there are no easy ways of deciding how much time to spend with whom, and for what purpose.

Our diagnostic tool helps people think about this spectrum of discretionary relationships with a fresh pair of eyes. They realise that they are over-reliant on a narrow category of people, and are missing out on opportunities further afield. Some concentrate only on relationships inside their company, or on people they see very regularly. Others focus too much outside and don't take the time to cement relationships with sponsors or influencers inside their organisation. Sometimes relationships with people they think of as supporters are stale and out-of-date.

The diagnostic tool helps people become aware of the limitations of their current relationships. It prompts a realisation that something needs to change. But they often say:

*So I'm not surrounding myself with the right people.*
*What do I do about it?*

We wrote this book to answer the question of what to do about it. The book is a reference guide for the people we work with in our coaching and leadership development. If you are wondering how to surround yourself with the right people, we hope you will find it useful.

## What is different about this book?

This book will introduce you to the idea of having a Personal Boardroom. It will help you choose a few individuals from amongst the many people you know professionally and personally. They will not all be drawn from your most intimate or frequent relationships—you will include a few distant people you see infrequently. Some of the people you choose for your Personal Boardroom will be different from you, so that they connect you with new ways of seeing your world as it is now, and anticipating what is to come. Others will be close enough to you and work to provide frank feedback and direct challenge, and to anchor you to what is important.

*The book describes 12 roles you need for your Personal Boardroom, and suggests how to pick people for each role.*

In a corporate boardroom, there are certain people you would expect to find at the table, such as the CEO and the CFO. If any one role is missing, a board meeting is incomplete. In the same way, a Personal Boardroom has a series of roles that need to be filled if it is to be effective: Customer Voice, Expert, Inspirer, Navigator, Unlocker, Sponsor, Influencer, Connector, Improver, Challenger, Nerve-Giver, and Anchor. The book offers tactics for recruiting people, assigning them to roles, and initiating useful conversations.

We are not the first to suggest that you can benefit from having a personal board of advisers. Jim Collins, author of *Good to Great*, put forward the idea of a personal board of advisers[2], and that term, or 'personal board of directors' has been widely used by others. There are also various movements that people associate with personal boards of directors, such as Lean In groups[3], YPO Forums[4], True North Groups[5] and Mastermind Groups[6]. These advocate bringing together a close-knit cluster of people who support each other personally and professionally.

*We are not the first to suggest that you can benefit from having a personal board of advisers.*

The Personal Boardroom approach is different in the following ways:

### It is structured.

You will think systematically about who in your network can help you—including both people you know well and with whom you can be truly honest (as the movements like True North Groups encourage), and peripheral people who are just as important, but for different reasons.

### It is action-oriented, purposeful and makes asking straightforward.

Rather than talking about 'support' in an unspecified way, our approach breaks down the different kinds of support you need into manageable elements (the twelve Personal Boardroom roles). That makes it easier to think about how different things can be provided by different people, leading to purposeful and focused conversations. This structure also makes it easy to ask for help.

### It is visual and measurable.

The book examines the overall composition of your Personal Boardroom and explains how to think about diversity and balance. It suggests ways to map and score your Personal

Boardroom so that you can see where there are gaps, or where you are over-reliant on certain people or types of people.

## It helps you to use your time well.

If you have time for the intense, mutual sharing in a True North or a Lean In group we have no doubt that it will reap great rewards for you. But these groups won't provide all the help you need, and they are not for everyone. At the other end of the spectrum, numerous online tools exist to help you keep track of your connections, and to add new ones. But there are few tools that can help you select, from the spectrum of connections you have, how to invest time with other people selectively in a way that will help you succeed in your career and as a leader of your business. In this book, you will find a way to make those selective investments in a purposeful way.

## It is focused on you, but creates freedom to help others.

Your Personal Boardroom is designed by you, for you. Its members are people you choose, for your own reasons. You draw in help from them, and you do not necessarily expect them to talk to or support each other (as you would in a True North or a Mastermind group). But this is not all about taking from others. The Personal Boardroom empowers you to benefit from others, while at the same time being a giver yourself.

These five characteristics—structured; action-oriented; visual and measurable; purposeful; and focused on both give and take—are what make our approach unique. And there is one other important aspect of this book:

## It brings to life academic research findings about the network characteristics of high performers.

The ideas in this book originate from academic research conducted by scholars in the US and the UK. This research demonstrates that people at the top of the performance distribution cultivate a small group of high-quality relationships that span physical boundaries and hierarchical levels.[7] Research also shows that, while a single relationship with a mentor or sponsor can explain short-term outcomes such as work satisfaction, it is the composition and quality of a set of relationships that account for long-run career outcomes like promotion.[8] The implication is that it is not sufficient to look to a boss, or a senior mentor or sponsor, to support you in your career and as a leader. High performers benefit from a constellation of high-quality relationships.[9]

*Research shows that it is not sufficient to look to a boss, or a senior mentor or sponsor; you need to build a set of high-quality relationships to drive and sustain success.*

Drawing on insights from this research, and from our work with hundreds of executives, this book shows how to create a constellation of high-quality relationships that will make a difference in your career, and to your success as a leader or a future leader. Its insights apply whether you are in a majority group (where 'majority' is defined by gender, ethnicity, nationality, age, sexual orientation or any other category) or in a minority. We believe the principles in this book apply to every leader in business today, so we do not lay out a special approach for people in minority groups. However, if that applies to you, we hope you too will discover the value these principles offer.

*This book offers a structured way to involve others in your career and your success, whoever you are.*

The book will also help you provide the guidance and support that other people, including those in minority groups, are looking for from you. You will identify where the unique value is that you can bring to people around you, to make your organisation, your team and your leadership a richer resource for others.

## A chapter-by-chapter overview

**Figure 1**, overleaf, is a route map for the book. You will find it repeated at the beginning of each chapter, as a signpost. Each chapter closes with a summary of the most important points.

If you have the opportunity to complete your own Personal Boardroom diagnostic, we encourage you to do so before you read this book, to establish a baseline against which you can judge progress.[10]

**Chapter 1** gives you a summary of the five steps involved in designing and building a Personal Boardroom. If you only have time for one chapter, make it Chapter 1. Once you've worked through its five steps, you will have an overview of what the rest of the book covers. If you are action-oriented and time-poor, Chapter 1 will give you enough to crack on with building your Personal Boardroom and having conversations with purpose.

**Chapter 2** takes a step back and considers the reasons for having a Personal Boardroom. It argues that a Personal Boardroom brings influence when you cannot rely on authority; extends your capability; provides a recourse when you cannot confide in your boss or colleagues; and enables you to connect from a place of strength, even when things are changing around you.

If you would like to work through the process of designing your Personal Boardroom in a structured, deliberate way, start with **Chapter 3**, which invites you to define a goal for your Personal Boardroom. Deciding on a goal will help you identify which of the twelve Personal Boardroom roles are most important to you, and who might fill them. And once you have decided what role you want someone to play, that role will provide a purpose and a focus for conversations.

Figure 1: A route map for the book

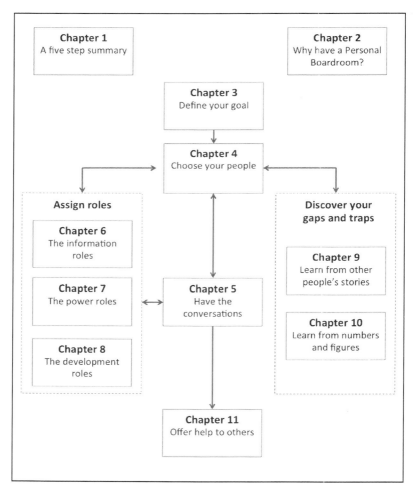

Once you are clear on a goal, **Chapter 4** helps you choose who should be in your Personal Boardroom. You will reflect on what a high-quality relationship is like, and consider what the overall composition and make-up of people in your Personal

Boardroom should be. You are aiming for a balanced group of people, drawn from both close and distant parts of your network, who between them provide a variety of viewpoints, and who can assist you in a range of different ways. Diversity is important too—both demographically, and in terms of the occupations, locations and work settings people are drawn from.

**Chapter 5** offers advice about how to choose people for your Personal Boardroom, and suggests ways to initiate conversations. It has tactics for how to recruit people, how to plan your approach, and how to make the first contact. It reviews different conversation strategies and considers how people vary in their orientations toward asking and giving. Chapter 5 also suggests how to make the most of the conversations and reflect on them.

Chapter 5 can be read alongside Chapters 6 to 8, which look in detail at the 12 roles in the Personal Boardroom. You might find these useful before diving into specific conversations. There are three groups of roles, as shown in Figure 2 oveleaf:

* **Information roles** (**Chapter 6**) provide access to knowledge, insights, perspectives and ideas you would not otherwise have.
* **Power roles** (**Chapter 7**) enable you to reach people and opportunities you would not otherwise be able to access, and to get things done.
* **Development roles** (**Chapter 8**) give you the self-knowledge to be better at what you do, and to come across at your most powerful to others.

Chapters 6 to 8 describe each role and the characteristics of people who are likely to be suited to each type of role. They invite you think about what is implicit when you ask for help, and offer some questions to check that you have identified the right people.

Figure 2: The 12 Personal Boardroom roles

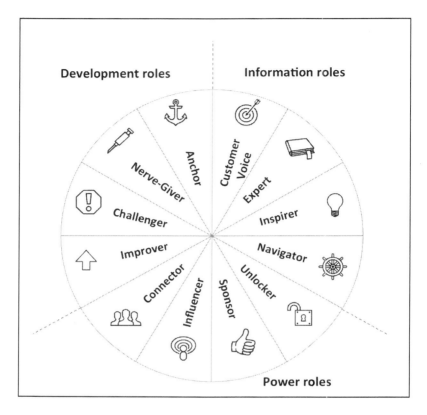

In our work with people on their Personal Boardrooms we observe traps that people often fall into, and gaps and biases caused by relying too much on one type of person, or one individual, or on relationships that are no longer relevant to today's challenges. Using stories from people we have worked with, **Chapter 9** recounts some of these patterns—the bingo boss, the empty Boardroom, the inside Boardroom, the outsider, the stale Boardroom, the outpost, and the inherited Boardroom—and suggests what to do if one of these applies to you.

**Chapter 10** shares some of the metrics and figures we use, so that you can carry out a Personal Boardroom diagnosis for yourself. If you like to quantify things and to think visually, Chapter 10 is for you. Its analytical tools can help you sense-check whether you are making good decisions about who you surround yourself with.

Finally, **Chapter 11** suggests how to use the Personal Boardroom framework to be an initiator of generosity for others, using the Personal Boardroom roles as a structure for contributing to the careers of others in a purposeful way. The idea of offering as well as asking is an important part of our framework. We believe that your leadership, your career and your business will be stronger if you are willing to both ask for help and to offer it to others.

## Three things you need to believe to use this book

There are just three things you need to believe to make use of the ideas in this book. They are:

*1. No one need go on a career journey alone.*

Your career is a journey of one. No one started where you started, and then took identical steps to you. Your career is uniquely yours. But, the stories we often hear about success are stories of individual heroism, about how people made it by private genius and dogged self-belief. The reality is they succeeded on their journey by drawing the right people around them and receiving many helping hands along the way. The same applies to you. We developed the concept of a Personal Boardroom to help you involve other people in your own success, and make it easy to do so.

## 2. Other people are not only willing to help you, but are happy to do so.

There is something macho about corporate life in the 21$^{st}$ century which makes asking for help seem weak. And some of us are reluctant to impose our requests on others. But the wonderful thing about human relationships is that we are naturally drawn to giving as well as taking. Most people, most of the time, get pleasure from helping others succeed.

As you read this book, you will learn to think about the help you need at a very granular level. There are 12 roles people in your Personal Boardroom can play for you (see Figure 2). From these roles, conversations will follow very naturally. You won't feel weak or self-serving. The network you need to succeed in your career—beginning with people in your Personal Boardroom and then extending beyond that group—will emerge organically from these conversations.

## 3. Asking for help goes hand-in-hand with offering it.

There are many books on influence techniques that emphasise the power of reciprocity. According to Robert Cialdini, *People say yes to those they owe*[11]. We like to think of it differently. When you ask a Personal Boardroom member, or anyone else, for help, it will not always be possible to reciprocate directly. But that should not matter, because there will be someone who you *can* help. If you are willing to 'pay it forward', your contribution will feed into a bigger community—whether that's the leadership tier of your business, the next generation of graduate recruits, a networking group you belong to, or the young unemployed in your town—in a way that make makes that community richer.

Our hope is that, in the conversations you have in the next few days and weeks, you will start to spot opportunities to offer career help to others, and that the vocabulary of the 12 roles will become a natural way to start conversations and talk about the help you can offer. By doing so, you will contribute to an ecosystem in which people support each other where they can, and seek help when they need to.

*Our vision is that you, and millions of executives like you, will form your own Personal Boardroom to help you become the leader you want to be, and that you will be an initiator of generosity for others.*

# 1 A five step summary

*The nice thing about all of this is that we can do it today.*

Sheryl Sandberg[12]

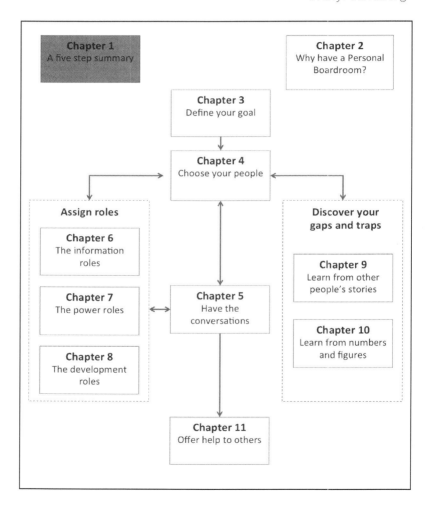

If you only have time to read one chapter, make it this one.

This chapter gives a rapid overview of how to design and build your Personal Boardroom, how to activate value from the people in it, and how to initiate acts of giving to others. If you are the kind of person who simply wants to get on and do things, this chapter is for you. It summarises the process of designing your Personal Boardroom in five steps.

If you need further reference points as you get going, the chapter also mentions where you can find further material in other parts of the book.

## The five steps: an overview

Imagine you are standing outside the door to a boardroom, and on it there is a sign written in your handwriting. This sign states what you want to achieve in that room. People enter your Personal Boardroom to help you toward that specific goal.

There are five steps involved in creating your Personal Boardroom:

Step 1: Define what your Personal Boardroom is for

Step 2: Choose 6–12 people for your Personal Boardroom

Step 3: Assign roles to the members of your Personal Boardroom

Step 4: Have the conversations

Step 5: Offer help to others

More details about each step follow. As you read on, bear in mind that this is an iterative process. Expect to go back and forward between the steps. As you start talking to members of your Personal Boardroom in Step 4, you might discover new people for Step 2, or you might want to assign a new set of roles in Step 3. You might realise that the goal you set for your Personal boardroom needs to change, so you go back to Step 1.

## Step 1: Define what your Boardroom is for

What do you want the people in your Personal Boardroom to help you achieve? If you understand this, everything that follows—whom you choose, which roles you assign to whom, how you have conversations—will have a purpose to it.

The result of Step 1 is a goal for your Personal Boardroom. It should not be more than 15 words. And it should be sticky. By sticky we mean it should be something that you can remember, and something that motivates you and gives you energy.

You are aiming to complete this sentence:

| My Personal Boardroom will help me to ...  *be the best 'ME' there is.* |
| --- |

When deciding what your Personal Boardroom is for, you can pick either a personal career goal, or something you want to achieve on behalf of your business. There are three broad categories of Personal Boardroom goal:

- Become the best leader I can be.
- Tackle a specific challenge or transition.
- Define my purpose as a leader.

The first of these is about aspiring to excellence. Your Personal Boardroom is there to inspire, challenge and empower you to become the best leader you can be, to provide you with creative insight, expertise and self-knowledge, to connect you with people who can help you get things done, to shore up your courage and help you cope with setbacks, and to remind you what you stand for. Chapter 3 suggests how to pick your people with this goal in mind, and how to establish a set of high-quality relationships that are optimised for the benefits they bring.

The second type of goal is results-focused, targeted at a specific personal or business objective or challenge. There is a list of examples in Chapter 3. For this type, you will recruit people into your Personal Boardroom who can help you meet that particular objective, so the goal will be very important in determining whether you have the right people, and what roles you want them to play.

The third goal type is about understanding your purpose as a leader and communicating a set of values and a vision that inspires others. If you are not clear on your purpose as a leader, a Personal Boardroom is the ideal place to start. A small group of people you trust can help you consciously develop and articulate what you stand for as a leader and to make that real. Chapter 3 gives further guidance on how to work with a Personal Boardroom to develop your purpose as a leader.

## Step 2: Choose people

The result of Step 2 is your best guess at the 6–12 people you want in your Personal Boardroom, given the goal you've chosen. The list may well change in Step 3, but it's useful to have a starting point. You are aiming to complete this sentence:

The members of my Personal Boardroom are …

You can do this in a two-stage process, in which you first generate a long-list and then narrow it down to 6–12 names.

## Generating a long-list

Your aim is first to generate as many possible candidates for your Personal Boardroom as possible. At this point, try not to worry about whether they are realistic choices. Generating a long-list without judging it will push your brain to come up with people you might not otherwise think of. Include people you know only distantly, and second-degree connections that you are aware of. (Second-degree connections are people known to contacts of yours, who you do not personally know.)

In Chapter 4 we suggest a practical exercise that will help to generate this long-list, called 'Should, Could, Might':

- Who **should** be in your Personal Boardroom?
- Who **could** be in your Personal Boardroom?
- Who **might** be in your Personal Boardroom?

The **should** people are the obvious ones to include, like your boss or mentor. The **could** people are those who you can identify as valuable. The **might** people are the more unusual possibilities, and the people you would include if you were being your most ambitious.

You can do this exercise in a general way or, once you are familiar with the 12 roles you need in your Personal Boardroom (see Step 3) you can do it with a specific role in mind.

## Narrowing down to 6–12 names

Look at each name in the long-list in turn, and sort them into groups.

This is where you need to think carefully about your relationship with each person. You want people who are likely to be interested in helping you succeed; though there are some exceptions to this, such as people who could act in the Challenger role (see Step 3).

It may feel easier to ask for help from close ties—people who you know well and trust. That is especially true when you are asking for feedback or for sponsorship. However, distant ties—people you don't see very often or do not feel close to—can be very valuable for gaining fresh information, and may be able to link you to a wider range of people.

In Chapter 4 we go into detail about how to choose members of your Personal Boardroom. There are some baseline rules that need to be met, and beyond that, we help you think about high-quality relationships. It is possible to have a high-quality relationship with someone you don't know well and see infrequently.

For now, aim for a shortlist of people you feel able to approach for help. Once you have a list of 6–12 names, step back for a moment. How does the overall composition look? Is there a predominance of certain types of people? In this book, we encourage you to think about diversity and balance. Diversity of age, gender, *etc.* is relevant, but there are other kinds of diversity that are more important: diversity in terms of career background; a mix of seniors, peers and juniors; a mix of people inside and outside your organisation; and a spread of people geographically.

## Step 3: Assign roles

The result of Step 3 is an assignment of roles to the 6–12 people in your Personal Boardroom. You do not need a direct mapping of one person per role. People can play more than one role, and roles can be played by more than one person. But you are aiming to have at least one role assigned to each person, and at least one person assigned to each role.

Figure 3: The 12 Personal Boardroom roles

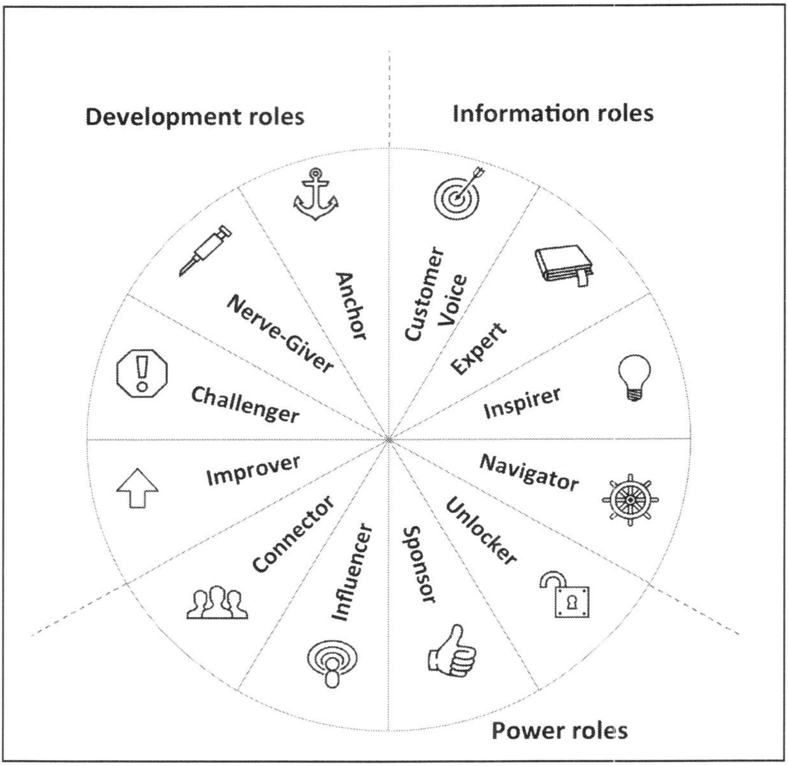

Below is a brief description of each role.

*Information roles*

- **Customer Voice** – someone who helps you understand markets, customers and business opportunities
- **Expert** – someone who gives advice based on their sector, or challenge-specific expertise
- **Inspirer** – someone who inspires new ideas and brings fresh thinking
- **Navigator** – someone who can tell you who you need to know, who does what and how things work

*Power roles*

- **Unlocker** – someone who provides access to resources (*e.g.* money, data, people's time)
- **Sponsor** – someone who speaks out to endorse you and your ideas to senior or important people
- **Influencer** – someone who works behind the scenes to win support, and helps you get things done
- **Connector** – someone who makes introductions and connects you with people who can help you

*Development roles*

- **Improver**—someone who gives candid, constructive feedback on your performance and development
- **Challenger**—someone who challenges your decisions and thinking, and helps you see your errors and blind spots
- **Nerve-Giver**—someone who strengthens your resolve at difficult times and gives you a sense of purpose
- **Anchor**—someone who keeps you grounded and holds you to account for the balance between your work and the rest of your life

You can find more detail on roles, with examples, in Chapter 6 for information roles; Chapter 7 for power roles; and Chapter 8 for development roles.

To assign roles to members of your Personal Boardroom, draw a grid like the one overleaf and label each cell as shown. Write the initials of anyone who plays that role for you, or could play that role in the future, in the relevant box.

As you go through this process for each of the people you picked, you may find that some roles are unfilled. Go back to your list of names to see if there is anyone you could add for these roles.

Table 1: Assigning roles to members of your Personal Boardroom

| Information Roles | Power Roles | Development Roles |
|---|---|---|
| Customer Voice | Unlocker | Improver |
| Expert | Sponsor | Challenger |
| Inspirer | Influencer | Nerve-Giver |
| Navigator | Connector | Anchor |

Check the list of 6-12 people from Step 2. If a person on your list from Step 2 is not assigned to any role, should they be? And if they do not fill any of the roles, what is it that they do for you, or could provide for you?

You may find that you start adding people, so that the number of people in your Personal Boardroom creeps up over 12. We set a limit of 12 for a reason. You need to invest time and attention to make these relationships work for you, but your capacity to invest in Personal Boardroom relationships is not limitless. A Personal Boardroom comprising 12 people is large enough to cover all of the roles, but not so large that it takes up all of your time. In Chapter 4 we suggest various ways to work out the optimal combination of people and roles. Your goal is to establish a set of high-quality relationships that is balanced in terms of where people are drawn from, and offers a blend of diverse and familiar perspectives.

Once you have completed Step 3, count up the number of roles each person plays. Does one person dominate? Sometimes people have a boss who fills all the roles. We call this person a 'bingo boss'. That's a great boss to have, but you are vulnerable if that person moves on. Chapter 9 suggests what to do if you have a bingo boss, or one of a several other common patterns: the empty Boardroom, the inside Boardroom, the outsider, the stale Boardroom, the outpost, and the inherited Boardroom

## Step 4: Have the conversations

This is the point at which the process moves from planning to action, and you make your Personal Boardroom real.

The result of Step 4 is a series of conversations in which you issue a request for help, and reflect on the outcome.

How you manage these conversations depends on you and your personality and motivation, the people you have chosen, and the roles you want them to play. Chapter 5 will help you to choose the right conversation strategy for you, and to decide how to approach people.

*There is one golden rule:*
*your conversations must be purposeful.*

Use the goal you identified in Step 1 and the role assigned to each person in Step 3 to make your request. Somewhere in the email or the conversation, you are going to weave in a request like this:

I am aiming for/taking on/thinking of/hoping to …

[Insert here the goal you identified for your Personal Boardroom.]

I wondered if you would help me by acting as a …

[Insert here the role you want the person to play.]

… by …

[Explain what you want them to do, and make it specific to the role.]

## Step 5: Offer help to others

The Personal Boardroom is a tool for you to give help to others, as well as to ask for it. Those others include members of your Personal Boardroom. But don't think only about how to reciprocate to those 12 people. Also think about others you could help, who are not in your Personal Boardroom, but who could benefit from you.

The result of Step 5 is a list of people you could provide help to; and for each person on that list, a role you could play. Look at the list of roles in Step 3. Is there a role you excel at? Keep this role in mind as you generate the list.

Pick three names from the list. Then go and have the conversations. Take the initiative to make the approach. You cannot invite yourself into their Personal Boardroom—that is for them to decide. But you can offer your help. In Chapter 11 we talk more about why offering help is important, and suggest that you consider becoming a specialist in one or more of the 12 roles as a giver.

## Summary of Chapter 1

Step 1: Define what your Personal Boardroom is for.

Step 2: Choose 6–12 people for your Personal Boardroom.

Step 3: Assign roles to the members of your Personal Boardroom.

Step 4: Have the conversations.

Step 5: Offer help to others

# 2 Why have a Personal Boardroom?

*'That's the hard thing about hard things—there is no formula for dealing with them.'*

Ben Horowitz, technology CEO and investor [13]

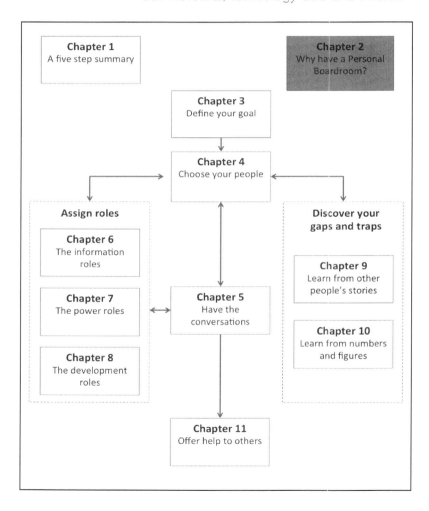

Ben Horowitz, technology entrepreneur and Silicon Valley investor, knows just how *really hard* it is to be a leader.[14] Building a high-tech company when no one understood the Internet; raising investment when the economy was in melt-down; leading a group of people out of trouble; and motivating people when the business had 'turned to crap': these are the some of hard things that Horowitz has dealt with in his leadership career.

And although there is no formula for dealing with the hard things, in his book *The Hard Thing about Hard Things*, Ben Horowitz offers some pieces of advice for how to survive as a CEO. His first piece of advice is this: make some friends.

In the book, Horowitz repeatedly alludes to the friends who helped him survive. There was Marc Andreessen, who began as his boss at Netscape, and with whom he co-founded Loudcloud (later Opsware), and Andreessen Horowitz. Of Andreessen he says: 'Even after eighteen years, he upsets me almost every day by finding something wrong in my thinking, and I do the same for him. It works.' [15]

There was John O'Farrell, the greatest 'big deals person' Horowitz ever knew, and Mark Cranney, a sales expert with an extraordinary knowledge of the deals Opsware was competing for. Michael Ovitz, the most powerful dealmaker in Hollywood, gave shrewd advice on negotiation, and 'networking guru' Ron Conway forged a vital connection to Herb Allen of Allen & Company, who became a loyal investor.

Bill Campbell's acerbic wisdom gave Horowitz the nerve to push ahead with an IPO when the market was tanking. Andy Rachleff, investor, was a brilliant abstract thinker. A client, Frank Johnson (not his real name), was a vital gatekeeper to an important relationship with EDS. Horowitz's father reminded him that flowers are cheap and divorce is expensive. His wife Felicia urged him to push on with an IPO roadshow even as she recovered from a medical emergency.

Without using the term, Ben Horowitz's book described the Personal Boardroom that helped him to not only *survive* the hard things, but also to *succeed* as CEO of a technology venture that he co-founded, ultimately selling it to Hewlett Packard for $1.6 billion.

> *A Personal Boardroom is a small group of people—typically from 6 to12—who help you succeed.*

To understand the concept of a Personal Boardroom and how it operates, think about a corporate boardroom. That is a place where a CEO and the executive team are held accountable for their actions by investors and their representatives. However, a good corporate board, with carefully selected non-executive directors, offers much more than simply keeping the team accountable.

Board members bring in expertise that the executive team do not have. They challenge decisions, and offer an honest appraisal of ideas and suggestions. They bring fresh insights and a different perspective, and provide introductions to useful people and access to resources. Board members can also bring reputational benefits and goodwill, and if relationships are positive they can provide support and help the executive team recover from setbacks. The conversations that bring these benefits often take place outside of formal meetings.

The same principles apply to a Personal Boardroom. A good Personal Boardroom provides expertise you don't have, like John O'Farrell did for Ben Horowitz. Its members speak out on your behalf and unlock resources, as Frank Johnson did for a deal that represented 90% of Opsware's revenues. They help navigate situations you are not familiar with (Mark Cranney), and make introductions (Ron Conway and Michael Ovitz). They provide feedback, and challenge your thinking to make it better (Marc Andreessen and Bill Campbell). They remind you why you do what you do (Felicia Horowitz). They also keep you true to who you are and look after your wellbeing (Horowitz's father).

A Personal Boardroom allows you to move beyond relying only on yourself, your boss, and—if you're  lucky—a mentor or coach. It reduces the vulnerability of being dependent on your board of directors. Having a Personal Boardroom means you can draw routinely on insights from people further afield, like customers who offer insights into target markets, or colleagues in the global headquarters. And it assuages the feeling of loneliness at the top of an organisation, by providing people to confide in when you cannot share things with your boss, peers, or direct reports.

*A Personal Boardroom assuages the feeling of loneliness at the top of an organisation.*

As you navigate complicated organisations and markets, and coordinate partnerships to get things done, the people in your Boardroom can help you understand who is powerful and important. They provide access to informal power by connecting you to people who are not outright decision-makers or budget-holders, but who nonetheless have influence because their views are respected by those who are.

*A Personal Boardroom brings influence when you cannot rely on authority.*

Your Personal Boardroom can help you respond quickly and with insight in an environment overloaded with information. You can't know everything, but your Boardroom makes it possible to draw on experts to decode complex information and speed up decision-making. As the pace at which your business develops and delivers new products and services increases, being able to turn to people you trust who can quickly appraise your ideas, challenge your arguments and test your solutions is ever more important.

*A Personal Boardroom extends your capability by providing speedy access to people with expertise different from yours.*

Finally, a strong Personal Boardroom enables you to connect from a place of strength and purpose, even when things are changing all around you. Boardroom members who thrive on reinventing things and are in touch with the next new thing can introduce you to new ideas and innovations, fuelling your capacity to keep pace with change. People who are connected with different audiences from your own can provide fresh perspectives and link you to new connections. Strong, safe relationships help you connect with the real you, and to be true to your values as a leader. They give you courage to deal with the hard things, enable you to cope with shocks and setbacks, and renew your focus and energy.

*A strong Personal Boardroom enables you to connect from a place of strength and purpose, even when things are changing.*

This book shows how to design and build a Personal Boardroom that means you will not only survive, but will succeed, and thrive, in your job today. And when tomorrow's challenges arrive, the book will help you move on with grace to design and build the Personal Boardroom you need to meet those challenges too.

## Summary of Chapter 2

Being a leader involves hard things, and there are often no formulae for dealing with the hard things.

A Personal Boardroom is a small group of people—typically from 6 to 12—who help you not only survive the hard things, but also succeed as a leader.

There are four reasons for having a Personal Boardroom:

1.  It reduces the feeling of loneliness at the top, and when you can't confide in your boss or colleagues.

2.  Its members bring influence when you cannot rely on authority.

3.  It extends your capability

4.  It enables you to connect from a place of strength and purpose, even when things are changing around you

# 3 Define your goal

*People don't buy what you do.*
*They buy why you do it.*

Simon Sinek[16]

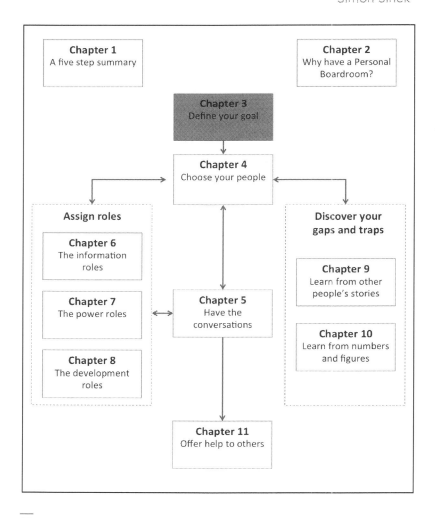

## The who, the how and the why

As you read through this book you will find plenty of practical advice about *who* and *how*: who to choose for your Personal Boardroom, and how to work with those people so you can be successful in your career, and as a leader of your business.

But at the heart of making the *who* and *how* work is having a good understanding of the *why*: why are you designing and building a Personal Boardroom, and what is it that you want the people in it to help you achieve?

*At the heart of an effective Personal Boardroom is a good understanding of what you want to achieve through it.*

Choosing a purpose or goal for your Personal Boardroom is personal: only you can decide. We have found that most people want their Personal Boardroom to help with one or more of the following:

1. Being the best they can be as a leader
2. Tackling a specific challenge or transition
3. Defining their purpose as a leader

The first—being the best you can be as a leader—is about striving for excellence. If you believe that leaders are only as good as the people they surround themselves with, then you might be drawn to this as a goal. You will look to your Personal Boardroom members to inspire you to excel in things you are good at; to provide creative insight, self-knowledge and expertise; to offer an outside perspective; to bring courage during hard times; to help you cope with setbacks; and to remind you what you stand for.

The second type of goal—tackling a specific challenge or transition—is focused on results. It will appeal to you if you are taking on a new role, looking for a promotion or a job move, or embarking on a major project or initiative. In any of these cases you are looking for a targeted contribution and involvement. You will select people for your Boardroom who can help you meet a very particular objective, possibly on a short-term basis. You might even decide you need several Personal Boardrooms, each focused on a different and specific aspect of your work.

The third type of goal—defining your purpose as a leader—is focused on meaning and values. It will appeal to you if you believe that great leaders can articulate what they stand for and excite others to share their vision. Inviting your Personal Boardroom members to help you define your purpose as a leader only works if you are willing to make it real. That could mean changes to your team or your organisation, or more personal changes to how you communicate, or allocate time, or even to what job you want to do. So this is an intimate goal, with potential to have a transformative effect; but be prepared for the consequences.

In the following sections we talk in more detail about each type of goal.

## Goal type 1: Excellence as a leader

Let's look at the analogy of preparing for a board meeting to bring this goal alive. At board meetings, the conversation is high-level and strategic, so you have to lift your nose from the day-to-day detail in order to prepare. At the meeting you know you'll be asked searching questions and be confronted with opinions that are different from yours. You expect to leave the meeting with renewed focus and direction, and with a demanding to-do list that will maximise the opportunities ahead. You hope also to leave the meeting knowing that the other people there will play their part to make things happen.

Organisations have board meetings for a variety of governance reasons. Aside from governance, there are also two ways in which board meetings can bring value. First, the need for preparation and being accountable creates discipline and a routine, and ensures things that should get done do get done. Second, a good meeting is a rubbing together of excellent people and great ideas that spark clearer thinking and cluster around a shared sense of purpose and momentum.

The primary value of a good board is actually delivered outside of formal meetings. Non-executive directors are often called on for *ad-hoc* advice; introductions are made; challenging conversations are held. Board members encourage and exhort the executive team. They celebrate and cajole, and wade in when necessary.

*A Personal Boardroom whose goal is excellence as a leader will lift your focus from operational detail, and help you anticipate the future.*

Ben Horowitz, technology CEO, wrote of one of his board members, Bill Campbell, that Bill was the kind of guy you called when you needed someone who would be really excited for you, and equally when things went horribly wrong. He described many times when Bill's advice was crucial. One was when Ben called Bill to let him know that their ailing company Loudcloud had been saved by a disposal to EDS. According to Horowitz, Bill replied: "'Too bad you can't go to New York and be part of the announcement …You need to stay home and make sure every employee knows where they stand … They need to know whether they are working for you, EDS, or looking for a fucking job.'"[17] And he was right, Horowitz said. Bill's out-of-meeting advice was as vital as any word he spoke during a board meeting.

Your Personal Boardroom can create value for you in just the same way. The people in it help you to be excellent as a leader, given the resources you have to work with, and the responsibilities you have to deliver. Your Personal Boardroom is unlikely to be involved in much operational detail. The members' job is to help you look over the parapet to anticipate the future; to think strategically; to head off poor decisions; and to recharge your batteries. They do this outside the daily detail of your job.

In that case the goal of your Personal Boardroom might be something like this:

My Personal Boardroom will help me to be the best I can be as a leader.

Or

My Personal Boardroom will help me to become the leader I want to be.

## Bearing this goal in mind as you pick people

If this is your goal for your Personal Boardroom, what should be foremost in your mind as you choose people and assign roles?

Of course, it is important to choose people you can trust, who will deliver on what they promise, and who make you feel energised. Beyond that, look for a balance between people who see your work from close quarters—including your boss, but also peers and direct reports—and people who can bring an outside perspective.

There are three roles that we have found to be critical in a Personal Boardroom whose goal is about leadership excellence.

 **Improvers** show you how you come across to others. They tell you how your behaviour and conduct are actually perceived. A leader who strives for excellence will include direct reports, or other junior colleagues, as Improvers, as well as a peer who can comment on the leader's tone and content in meetings, and their boss. Improvers reflect back the good, the bad and the ugly so that you can learn from them.

 **Customer Voices** provide insight into what your consumers, services-users or clients are thinking about your business or your team. A leader who strives for excellence will have more than one Customer Voice who is outside their company. If your immediate customers are internal, their voice needs to be heard in your Personal Boardroom too. It may also be important to hear the voices of other stakeholders like investors, employees or regulators.

 **Influencers** are people who provide behind-the-scenes support for your initiatives. They are respected for their views and opinions, although they are not always senior or in formally powerful roles. Leaders who strive to be excellent have Influencers who help them deliver results and create consensus where they do not have authority. Your Personal Boardroom needs Influencers who are not members of your team or your peer group. They are to be found in corporate HQ, in other countries or business units, in client organisations, or in other external organisations.

When you create a Personal Boardroom to help you be the best you can be as a leader, you are probably thinking about relationships that will endure for a year or more, rather than months or weeks. From time to time, it's inevitable that you will face a specific challenge that requires new expertise or the support of someone new. How do you deal with specific challenges if you see your Personal Boardroom as a committed group of people who are with you for the long haul?

Aim for a core of nine or ten long-standing members, and reserve one or two revolving seats to bring in required expertise from time to time.

Alternatively, if a very major transition or project comes along, you might choose to reconfigure your Personal Boardroom. In that case, you would be looking at the second type of goal, described in the next section.

# Goal type 2: Tackling a specific challenge

We recently came across this wonderful unattributed quote:[18]

> *Bite off more than you can chew.*
> *Then chew like hell.*

Let's say you want to introduce a more innovative culture into your business, or change the way finance is perceived in your organisation, or improve its record on diversity, or launch a new product line, or develop a strategy for digital transformation. What do you do? Do you expect to tackle this challenge by taking it on single-handedly and then chewing like hell?

Hopefully, the answer is no. You will invite your Personal Boardroom to help you.

In that case the goal of your Personal Boardroom might start like this:

My Personal Boardroom will help me as a leader in my business to [succeed in a particular domain or with a specific challenge].

The specific challenge might be business-related or personal. A few business examples are:

- Introduce a stronger culture of [*e.g.* safety, innovation, sustainability] in the organisation.

- Change the way [finance, HR, digital] is perceived in the organisation.
- Launch a new product line in [X].
- Develop a strategy for [digital, growth, divestment].
- Deliver year-on-year growth of X in the next 12 months.
- Get a successful listing on the stock exchange.
- Raise X in investment.
- Secure a major new client or win a pitch.
- Complete an acquisition or disposal.
- Make a successful entry into an emerging market.
- Develop a new product range.
- Plan and deliver a major restructuring.
- Cut X% of costs.
- Integrate an acquired company.

Some examples of more individual and career-related goals are:

- Get a Board-level appointment.
- Get a non-executive director role.
- Be promoted to [state the level or job you are aiming for].
- Build my reputation as a [add words here].
- Survive a restructuring with a better job at the end.
- Change jobs.
- Find a new job.
- Think through a career change.
- Achieve a better quality of life.

In either case your goal should be no more than 15 words. If it is more than 15 words, it will not be succinct enough to catch people's attention; and you may not remember it either. It needs to be something that is 'sticky'. A sticky goal is one that your find exciting and motivating, not just for the rewards it will bring you, but also because of the intrinsic pleasure and the satisfaction you'll get from progressing towards it.

Bear in mind that this kind of Personal Boardroom goal is a results-focused goal. You are asking people to help with something specific. What does success look like? Can you define a target or quantify an objective? If you can, the help you receive will be more focused.

## Bearing this goal in mind as you pick people

Given your goal for your Personal Boardroom, what should be top of your mind as you choose people and assign roles?

Here we outline some of the roles that we have found to be most important in a Personal Boardroom whose goal is result-oriented, and the typical profile for the kind of person who fills each role.

 **Navigators** are valuable for their deep exposure to situations that are unfamiliar to you, whether that be groups of employees, target consumers, new markets, government agencies or the like. They have an instinct for who the influencers are, and who it is useful to know. For business goals like changing culture, securing clients or entering new markets, Navigators understand the competitive landscape, and where the vested interests lie. Navigators are also helpful for personal goals like promotion or changing jobs, as they have a good insight into how decisions are made and who makes them. A results-focused Personal Boardroom will include Navigators who are familiar with the context, the politics, or the personalities affecting your specific challenge or transition.

**Challengers** are people who help you see your blind spots, sense-check your thinking, and improve your arguments. A results-focused Boardroom includes Challengers with enough experience of the specific issue you are taking on to be able to play their challenging role effectively. They make informed observations and ask probing questions thanks to prior familiarity with, or experience of, the same kind of issues you are now facing.

**Unlockers** are people who control budgets and access to resources, and **Influencers** are people who work behind the scenes on your behalf. A results-focused Boardroom includes Unlockers and Influencers with a direct involvement in the result you aspire to. If that is to pursue a new business opportunity, your Unlocker could be the person who provides you with a team to research a market or make the pitch, and an Influencer could be the person who is able to get you a meeting.

As always, it's important to have people you can trust, who will deliver and who bring energy. And while picking people, it is also important that you do not become so focused on your challenge that you lose sight of the value of diverse perspectives. We explore that further in the next chapter.

## Goal type 3: Defining your purpose as a leader

This third type of goal is very specific, like the previous type. We could have included 'define my purpose as a leader' in the list above as a personal goal, and left it at that. But we think this is worthy of special consideration for the following reasons:

Purpose is a tenet of good leadership. As Nikos Mourkogiannis says: *the real way to get ahead is to stand for something—to explicitly and consciously develop values that will coalesce into the kind of purpose that businesses can follow to succeed in today's world.*[19] An example is Paul Polman, who has transformed Unilever into a business driven by the following purpose: *We help people feel good, look good and get more out of life with brands and services that are good for them and good for others. We will inspire people to take small everyday actions that can add up to a big difference for the world. We will develop new ways of doing business that will allow us to double the size of our company while reducing our environmental impact.* [20]

If you are fortunate, you work in an organisation that has a clear sense of its own purpose, and that purpose both excites you and aligns well with your own values. If, like Polman, you are in a position to shape the purpose of that business, as a board-level executive or a business owner or entrepreneur, so much the better. But for many leaders, especially in large and complicated organisations, the organisation's purpose is not always something they can directly contribute to.

You still have a circle of influence, though.[21] That encompasses your team or the functional area you are responsible for, the division you service, or the country or region you manage. People within that circle look to you for guidance and inspiration. And outside that immediate circle, colleagues in other functions or geographies, partners, suppliers, and stakeholders are exposed to you and your work.

Your purpose is important because it energises you to get up in the morning; but even more so if it unleashes energy in others. However, coming up with a sense of purpose is not always easy, and nor is making it real in your day-to-day life. You might draft something on a piece of paper, but a purpose only moves others if it is factored into every decision and action you take.

*Boards of corporate enterprises are ultimately responsible for what those enterprises exist to do. Your Personal Boardroom can do the same for you as a leader.*

We think the Personal Boardroom concept is well suited to this particular goal, and to taking you on a journey to becoming a better leader. Boards of corporate enterprises are ultimately responsible for what those enterprises exist to do. Your Personal Boardroom can do the same for you as a leader. With the right people, assigned to the right roles and the right conversations, you will be able to crystallise how your life and your work matters; and with that clarity of purpose, to excite your team, your colleagues and the circles of people around you.

Do you know your purpose as a leader? Do you know why you do the work you do, and what you get out bed for? Can you explicitly and consciously articulate those values for your team, for other people to buy into? Would you like to be able to? If so, the goal of your Personal Boardroom might be:

> My Personal Boardroom will help me define what I stand for as a leader.

## Bearing this goal in mind as you pick people

If this is your goal for your Personal Boardroom, what should be on top of your mind as you choose people and assign roles?

Here we touch on just three roles that we have found to be important in a Personal Boardroom whose goal is about meaning and purpose.

**Anchors** are people who remind you who you are and what you stand for (in life and work) and are concerned for your well-being. Anchors are often spouses and family members, and this is vital if you are to keep all of the domains of your life—especially the one outside work—in balance as you think through your purpose as a leader. It is equally important, however, that your purpose-led Boardroom includes Anchors drawn from your professional life: people who know you as a colleague; who can reflect back to you their perceptions on where your edge lies and what makes you tick as a leader. It sometimes takes other people to let us know how we can be at our most powerful. [22]

**Inspirers** are people who buzz with new ideas and fresh thoughts. They are great at seeking things through a different lens from you. That includes opening your eyes to a new way of thinking about yourself, your career and what's important to you. While Anchors are a stabilising force, Inspirers do the opposite: they stretch your ambition to new heights or breadths, and breathe new life into your aspirations. They make you dare to believe more and to ask more of yourself and those around you.

**Nerve-Givers** provide the courage to make difficult decisions and carry them through. They fuel your belief that you are capable of delivering on the ambition, or living up to the values you have set yourself. They help with the hard parts too. A new sense of purpose may result in hard choices and disappointed people as a follow-through. To manage the turbulence that follows, Your Personal Boardroom needs to include Nerve-Givers who are able to remind you why this is happening, and help you stay on course.

Using your Personal Boardroom to define your purpose can be a powerful tool. Be aware that powerful tools have powerful effects. If you are interrogating what you stand for as a leader, the result might be a renewed conviction that you are doing the right thing. Then, your Personal Boardroom can help you best you can be as a leader. With that in mind, you might look back to the earlier section on leadership excellence as a Personal Boardroom goal.

But the consequence of defining your purpose might be a change in a career, or a downshifting decision, or a switch into a different functional area. It might be a decision to end a product line, to reallocate a resource, or to enter a new market. So, once your Personal Boardroom has helped you define your purpose, you may need to reconfigure it to help in a more specific way. In that case refer to the section above on challenge-specific Personal Boardroom goals.

## They buy why you do it.

In this chapter we have discussed three types of Personal Boardroom goal. But across all of the three types, there is one common and over-riding priority, which is to create a real buy-in from others about *why* this is important. Why does your particular goal—whether that's about being an excellent leader, or dealing with a specific opportunity to deliver a great result, or defining your purpose—matter to you, and why should others care about it?

In the same way, your conviction about the *why* for your Personal Boardroom can inspire willingness in others and ignite their motivation to help you. Personal Boardroom members who have been loyal supporters for a long time may be more than willing to help simply because they believe in you. For them, the fact that it's you may be enough of a *why*. But for others who know you less well, having a sense of purpose as a leader, and being able to clearly articulate that, will be an asset as you start to have the conversations with them.

*Being clear about your goal will inspire willingness in others and ignite their motivation to help you.*

In Chapter 5 we discuss how to recruit people for your Personal Boardroom, with some very practical suggestions. More than anything else, however, being able to generate a shared sense of purpose—that this is not just about you and your ambitions, but about them and you creating something together that goes beyond you—is the most important ingredient for a vibrant Personal Boardroom.

## Summary of Chapter 3

The heart of making a Personal Boardroom work is having a good understanding of what you want it to achieve.

There are three types of Personal Boardroom goals:

1. Be the best you can be as a leader.

2. Tackle a specific challenge or transition.

3. Define your purpose as a leader.

If you can get across to others why your goal is important to you, and create a vision of what you can achieve together, this will make for a vibrant Personal Boardroom.

# 4 Choose your people

*One of the things I really stress in casting is I need to find someone who is suitable for the role.*

Stephen Chow, film director[23]

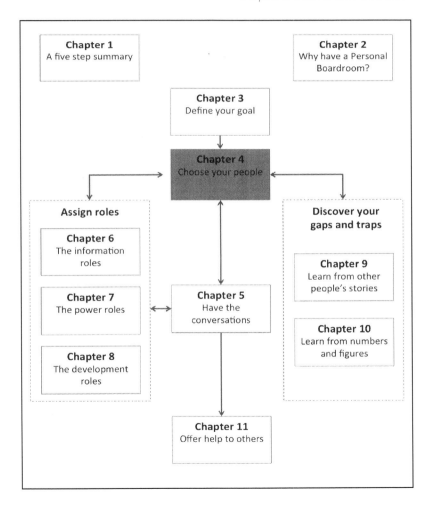

This chapter is about casting for your Personal Boardroom It will be particularly useful if any of the following apply:

- You have been thinking about who should be in your Personal Boardroom for the first time, either while reading Chapter 1 and acting on its five steps, or by using our diagnostic tool. This was new territory and you started asking yourself new questions about who you surround yourself with.
- One of the two chapters on spotting your gaps and traps has caused a rethink. Chapter 10 suggested ways you can undertake a diagnostic process for yourself using your own mapping and metrics, and Chapter 9 told stories about other people's Personal Boardrooms. Reading either of those chapters, you realise you are over-reliant on certain types of people, or you have gaps you would like to fill.
- Chapter 3 has helped you decide on a goal for your Personal Boardroom, and you want to configure a set of high-quality relationships that will help you achieve that goal.

If any of these apply, this chapter will help you.

But there is something else you might be struggling with, a constraint we imposed on you: we only let you have up to 12 people. So let's start with that.

## Why 6–12 people?

In our experience, people's capacity to invest in Personal Boardroom relationships is finite. What do we mean by 'invest'? We mean spending time in conversation with your Boardroom members; following up on actions they suggest; keeping them up to date with progress; and staying in touch with what is going on for them, in their team or business or market. All of these actions—including the last one—are needed if you are to make each of them feel valued and important to you.

We also think the number of people in your Personal Boardroom should be limited to twelve because you want an optimal return on the time you spend. You want to spend enough time listening and learning to have genuinely new insights, but not so much time that you become paralysed by too much advice, or by a huge to-do list.

*Twelve is the optimum number to deliver all the resources you need without consuming excessive amounts of time.*

Perhaps you have the opposite problem. You can only think of a handful of people, and even six feels like a stretch. You might know lots of people, but few qualify for something that sounds as strategic or as intimate as a Personal Boardroom. If this is your situation, you might also be aware that there are role-gaps that need to be filled. If so, this chapter will help you think creatively about how to fill them.

The overall composition of your Boardroom matters too. Your Personal Boardroom will be most effective if you have some diversity in the range of people in it, and if you avoid relying too heavily on certain individuals or categories. Later in this chapter, we suggest how to think about whether you have sufficient diversity.

## Who *Should, Could, Might* be in your Personal Boardroom?

If you followed the steps set out in Chapter 1 you'll remember that we encouraged you to generate a long-list of possible candidates for inclusion in your Personal Boardroom. Why did we do that?

It's easy for our brains to get locked into near-at-hand solutions, which are comfortable and involve little effort. For example, let's say you work in a team that is buried inside a large business unit, which itself is part of a large subsidiary of a global company. It's easy to think of your fellow team members, your boss, your boss's boss, and perhaps your direct reports, as possible members of your Personal Boardroom.

How far should you stray beyond your immediate team or business unit? What about the managing director's PA, or the people in an offshore operations team? You don't work directly together, but could there be reasons for including them? Generating a long list of names invites your brain to toy with the possibility that other people—and especially the non-obvious people—might be useful members of your Boardroom. As you read this, a voice inside your head might be saying *That's ridiculous! Why would the managing director's PA be in my Personal Boardroom?* But have you considered whether the PA could be a useful Navigator, or Influencer? Or a Challenger, telling you how the MD is likely to react to a suggestion you want to make?

*Generating a long list of names stretches your insight into who might be useful members of your Personal Boardroom.*

The point of generating a long-list of names is to stretch your brain to come up with as many ideas as possible and—here is the crucial bit—to try to suppress the judgmental voice telling you all the reasons why any particular name is stupid, or irrelevant, or unrealistic. Because the stupid ideas may well be stupid, but they might lead on to an idea that isn't stupid. Perhaps there is another PA who could be useful. Perhaps there is someone else who reports to the MD, with an interest in seeing your team succeed.

## Generating a general list of candidates

To help with this divergent thinking process, ask yourself three questions:[24]

**Who *should* be in my Personal Boardroom?** Think of all the obvious people—your boss, a sponsor or mentor, your boss's boss, the chair of the executive committee. These are people who already know and understand that they have a role to play in helping you to be successful. Most likely, they are strong ties: people you interact with frequently, and who work with the same people you work with. Consider other people you work with: your peers, executive team members, your direct reports, important customers or suppliers, *etc.*

**Who *could* be in my Personal Boardroom?** Widen the list to include people who provide you with information or advice in the course of doing your job: a lawyer, your HR partner, your management accountant, your operations team, *etc.* Think about former colleagues and bosses. What about other people in your industry, or someone doing something similar to you in another company? Think about weak ties—people you see infrequently, and who move in different social worlds, like heads of industry associations, or journalists in your sector. Include people outside your industry. Could friends or acquaintances help you—even if they are not in the same industry?

**Who *might* be in my Personal Boardroom?** To carry out this third part, dial up your ambition and put yourself in the shoes of a very successful version of yourself. Then widen the list. Who would you know? Who would be pleased to pick up the phone if you called? Or think about who is the most influential or successful person in your line of work, and the people he or she relies on or respects. Who do your competitors work with? Who will take over from your boss if she moves on?

The purpose of this exercise is to stretch your brain to come up with unlikely possibilities. Remember to suppress the judging voice while you are doing this. Yes, there may be reasons for rejecting some of these people; but resist the urge to rule people out until you have pushed yourself to generate a long-list.

## Generating a long-list to fill a specific role

If you are aware of certain role-gaps in your Personal Boardroom, you can repeat the Should, Could, Might exercise with a specific role in mind. For example, let's say you are aware that you don't have a Customer Voice, other than your boss.

**Who *should* be my Customer Voice?** Are there certain key individuals who pay the bills each quarter? Is there a primary or prominent customer in the market you serve who can represent their views? Is there a senior individual inside the business who is the direct beneficiary of your team's work?

**Why *could* be my Customer Voice?** Who are the main users of your product or service? Who pays for the product or service on their behalf? Is there an emerging customer category that you don't fully understand? Who can help you understand the demographic categories you serve (*e.g.* young consumers, the elderly, emerging market users, people in financial difficulty)?

**Who *might* be my Customer Voice?** Does it help to think about investors or shareholders as your customers? Is there a primary or prominent investor who can represent their views? Should regulators, government ministers, agencies, community groups, *etc.,* have a voice in your Personal Boardroom? Are there markets you haven't yet tapped, who might be customers in the future?

## Generating a list of go-betweens

As you go through this process, it may become obvious that you don't actually know anyone who can fill a role. Not yet, anyway.

In that case, create a career profile for the ideal person. If you need a Customer Voice, think about the industry, the type of company, the job title and responsibilities, and any specific career background that a helpful Customer Voice might be expected to have. For example, if your team is trying to persuade advertisers to spend less on TV advertising and more on digital search-and-displays ads, you might like to have a Chief Marketing Officer (CMO) as your Customer Voice.

How will you reach this person? That is where your Connectors and Navigators can be extremely powerful. The right Navigator would know the marketing landscape well enough to tell you about various CMOs. A Connector might be able to introduce you to one or two CMOs so that you can start to build a relationship. Connectors can be extremely powerful in creating a bridge to new parts of a network, especially if they are weak ties. They can be very useful go-betweens, helping you take a step towards reaching other people, so may deserve to be on your long-list simply for that.

*Weak ties are able to connect you with new parts of a network and to expose you to creative insights*

Ties with people outside your social group, and to people who interact with a different set of people from you, are known as weak ties. Such interactions are likely to be infrequent and not especially close, but they have enormous value. Weak ties generate novel information, and create bridges to new parts of a network, and to people you don't yet know. And research shows that spanning between different social worlds can be a fertile source of creativity.[25] So, as you go through this divergent thinking process, think about weak ties who could be Connectors, Navigators or Inspirers.

Once you have generated your long-list of names, you have completed the divergent thinking exercise. Now, you can allow the judgmental voice to have its say as you begin a process of convergent thinking to narrow down your options. Below are several different ways of thinking about who should make the cut and be included in your Personal Boardroom:

## Do they meet the baseline rules?

Let's start with a few baseline rules for a Personal Boardroom relationship. It might surprise you, but we think you can include people you do not know very well, and people you do not trust absolutely; but only if they have these baseline characteristics.

First, **the person knows you and your work**. You have had some contact in the past—whether online, by phone or in person. Ideally, this includes a one-on-one conversation.

This does not mean you have to know the person intimately, or to spend masses of time together. Distant people who you don't see frequently can be considered as Boardroom members. In fact it's a good idea to include some distant people. The important thing, for more distant relationships, is that you make accurate and timely information available to them when they need it to play their role effectively.

> *Distant people, who you do not see frequently, can be considered as Boardroom members.*

Second **you trust them**. This doesn't mean that you would reveal your deepest flaws, or that you would expect to share proprietary or confidential information with them. But it does mean you trust their judgment and their expertise as it pertains to the role you want them to play; and that you are confident that they would follow up on any commitments, and would not misuse any information you share.

If there are people on your long-list who you don't fully trust, you don't have to reject them. There are plenty of people in commercial life with conflicting agendas, such as peers competing for the next promotion, budget owners who compete for limited funds, and people chasing the same clients. And there are people who make your life difficult, like awkward customers or demanding advisers. Such people can be great Challengers, and they can fill other roles too, such as Customer Voice, Expert and even Inspirer.

*You don't have to exclude people you don't fully trust, so long as you trust them in the role you have chosen for them.*

The important thing is that you trust their judgment and their expertise to deliver for you *in the role you want them to play*; and that, when the time is right, you feel able to ask them for help. In the next chapter we discuss the approach, and how to ask for help.

Third, **your relationship with them is current or emerging**. We often find when people do our Personal Boardroom diagnostic tool that they include former bosses. There can be good reasons for this: a supportive former boss can be a useful Sponsor, Influencer or Navigator. But sometimes people include former bosses because they haven't rebuilt an equivalent relationship with their current boss. When pushed, they admit that the old boss has little contact with their work now, and that actually they do not make any effort to keep up with them. We refer to this as a 'dormant' relationship.[26]

To identify whether a relationship is current or emerging, first think about when you last had one-to-one contact *via* email, phone, video conference, a social networking site or some other means. Then consider when you next plan to meet, and look at the list below:

- **Emerging** relationships: You recently met, or you recently started to get to know each other better. You expect to meet again, and that the contact between you will become more frequent in the future.

- **Current** relationships: You have been in touch recently, and your frequency of contact is growing or steady.
- **Dormant** relationships: You have not been in touch for a while, or your contact is sporadic. You met this person less often in the last year than in the previous year, or years. You do not expect to see them again anytime soon.

Current and emerging relationships have the benefit of freshness. The person will not be surprised to hear from you. Since you are in touch already, you should find an opportunity to work a Personal Boardroom request into the conversation. (See Chapter 5 for conversation strategies.)

> *It is easier to initiate Personal Boardroom requests in relationships that are current or emerging. Dormant relationships may need to be rekindled first.*

Dormant relationships need a bit of work, and once they are rekindled, you will need to invest time to keep the relationship current. Think about how natural it will feel to re-establish the relationship; will this person be pleased to hear from you, or surprised, or suspicious? In some cases, reigniting dormant relationships can take time, and you might want to include these on a list of people in your 'outer circle' who you want to get closer to.

## What category are they in?

Now that we've established the baseline rules for considering someone as a member of your Personal Boardroom, let's move on to some other factors you might take into account.

In this section of the chapter, we refer to the percentage of roles played by people in different categories. If you are the kind of person who likes the idea of scoring for your Personal Boardroom, Chapter 10 shows how to calculate this percentage, allowing for the fact that more than one person can play each role.

## Where are they drawn from?

We are sometimes asked whether it is OK to include people from outside the company. The answer is yes, of course. If you don't, how are you getting a perspective on how your customers think? Who is helping you look up from your day-to-day priorities to imagine the future?

If you work in a large or global organisation, there are five categories of people to include. In a small organisation, you may find that categories 2 and 3 do not apply exactly, but the principles remain the same.

1. **People in your team**: This category includes your direct reports.
2. **People in the same function or business unit, but not in your team**: This category includes your boss, peers who report to the same boss, and members of their teams. It also includes anyone else reporting directly to the same functional or business-unit head.
3. **People outside your functional or business unit, but in the same company:** This includes everyone in your company who reports to a different functional or business-unit head. In a matrix structure, it includes indirect bosses or reports. At Board level, this might include non-executive directors, and others concerned with the governance of the company.
4. **People in the same industry but a different company**: Include here anyone who works in your industry. These might be partners, suppliers or customers, depending on what they do. If it is hard to position your business in a particular industry, think of people whose organisations deliver a similar kind of product or service to yours.

5. **People outside the industry**: Suppliers, customers, a coach, your spouse or partner, family members, friends and former colleagues might appear here (unless they work in your industry).

We encourage you to choose at least one person from each category. We also suggest that people inside your company (categories 1 to 3) contribute no more than 70% of the roles, because of the benefits that an outside perspective can bring. People in categories 4 and 5 are usually weak ties (unless they are close friends or family members), and they will be able to connect you with both people and ideas from different walks of life.

## Where are they located?

Think about the physical location of the people on your list, and the workplace where they spend most of their time. There are four categories to consider:

1. People **who sit near you**, in the same office. This includes people whose desk or office you can easily wander past. You can also include in this category people you see every day, like family members.
2. People **in the same office, but who don't sit near you**. This includes people you're likely to bump into, on the way to a meeting room, the coffee machine or the water cooler.
3. People **who work in a different office** in the same country. For people in this category, you have to make an arrangement to meet up, so chance encounters are less likely.
4. People **who work in a different country**. Considerable effort has to be put in to keep these relationships current and to stay at the front of the other person's mind.

We encourage you to consider whether you are relying too heavily on people who are easy or convenient to reach. We think that people in the first two categories should fill no more than 50% of the roles in your Personal Boardroom.

You have to work harder to coordinate with people who work in different offices or countries, but a big advantage is that they will be less immersed in the same preoccupations as you, and more likely to have insights that are different from your own. They are more likely to be weak ties, helping you build bridges to different parts of your organisation, and places outside it. In a multi-national company, valuable connections to people in the corporate headquarters, and to heads of decision-making elsewhere, are typically in this category.

## How senior are they?

There are three categories to think about here:

1.  **People senior to you** in terms of their level and/or career attainment
2.  **Your peers**, and people you consider to be equivalent in career attainment
3.  **People junior to you**

Here, we encourage you to choose a spread of people across the three categories. Senior people are important, of course, but peers and direct reports can be very effective as Navigators, Improvers, Influencers, Challengers, Nerve-Givers, and in other roles. We suggest you aim for 30-50% of roles being filled by someone senior to you.

## How similar are they to you in career background?

It can also be useful to think about each person's education, and the industries and jobs they have been involved with in the past. Is their career background:

1.  **very similar** to yours?
2.  **fairly similar** to yours?
3.  **fairly different** to yours?
4.  **very different** to yours?

This can be hard to judge, especially if you don't know a person very well. However, what matters here is your perception. If you perceive that someone's background is similar or different to yours, that will determine how you interact, and what you look for from them.

Where people are similar to you, you'll benefit from a much higher level of common terminology, shared expectations and common experience. Communication will be easier, and this may be advantageous for giving feedback and offering expertise. Aim to have the majority of people in categories 3 and 4, because of the value that an outside perspective can bring.

*Think about creating a diverse Personal Boardroom, made up from people with a variety of backgrounds, and different levels of familiarity with your work, representing a range of stakeholders and organisations.*

All of the categories above help you think about creating a diverse Personal Boardroom, made up from people with a variety of backgrounds and different levels of familiarity with your work, representing a range of stakeholders and organisations. You might also like to think about the diversity of your Personal Boardroom in terms of demographic categories like gender, age, ethnicity and sexual orientation. The right proportions of people in each demographic category will be very personal to you, but if everyone in your Personal Boardroom is the same gender, age and ethnic background as you, you probably need to branch out.

## High-quality relationships

In addition to diversity across categories, a strong Personal Boardroom is made up of a set of high-quality relationships. What do we mean by high-quality?

## You energise each other

Imagine you are entering a room to have a conversation with a colleague. You spend the first ten minutes talking about how let down you feel by something that's happened. You moan that your boss doesn't like your ideas. Your colleague makes some suggestions about what you might do. You dismiss the suggestions, saying you don't believe things will change. Your phone rings half-way through the conversation and you lose your train of thought. When you finally get around to asking for help, how motivated do you think your colleague would be? Everything you have said and done has been de-energising.

Compare that with the idea of going into the room with an open mind, setting out your view of a problem, and then asking your colleague how they read the situation, and listening attentively to what they say. You acknowledge your boss's reasons for not liking your ideas. You build on your colleague's suggestions, and together you make sense of what has happened, and what you might do about it. Now, your colleague feels part of the solution, and has a shared interest in taking the next step with you. By bringing energy, you create a sense of mutual purpose and benefit that will bring out the best in others. [27]

*How you manage your interactions will have a powerful effect. By bringing energy, you create a sense of mutual purpose and benefit.*

There are of course two sides to this. Imagine instead entering a room to have a conversation with a member of your Personal Boardroom. Your colleague spends the first ten minutes complaining about something. When you finally get a word in—to mention that your boss doesn't like your ideas—your colleague criticises your ideas, and scoffs at the suggestion that your boss might change his mind. That is likely to be a de-energising conversation.

Not everyone is an energiser, so use this as a criterion to decide whom to choose for the Boardroom. Do they energise you? A de-energiser might be there for a good reason: as a vital Unlocker, a valued Expert, or a tuned-in Navigator. But, be aware of the positive value that energisers bring, and try to balance each de-energiser with an energiser in the same role.

*Balance any de-energisers in your Personal Boardroom*
*with an energiser in the same role.*

## You sustain momentum

Imagine having a conversation with a Boardroom member who agrees to do several things to help: making introductions, commenting on a business plan or a paper, mentioning your project to an important stakeholder, *etc.* You leave her office with a spring in your step. But the introductions don't come and the feedback never materialises. A few days pass and you send a reminder. You see her in the corridor; she looks guilty and promises again. A few weeks pass. Still no introduction or feedback. The important stakeholder doesn't seem to know about your project. By this time, the energy from that original conversation has dissipated.

*In a high-quality relationship you can rely on each other to*
*deliver on promises and commitments.*

Now imagine this situation the other way around. You promised some things to help your Boardroom member: following up on an introduction she made, finishing a paper that she agreed to comment on, providing a briefing for her, *etc.* She leaves the conversation feeling impressed. You let other things get in the way, or don't find time to do the things you promised to do. Again, the energy from the original conversation has dissipated.

A high-quality relationship is one where you trust each other to deliver on promises and commitments. You keep your Personal

Boardroom members up to date on your progress—and not just when you want something from them. You give them a sense of forward momentum, and they create it for you.

## Boundaries are respected

A high-quality relationship is one in which you feel safe. We talked earlier about trust, and said that a baseline requirement is that you feel able to ask for help, and that you trust the person's capability in the role you have chosen for them.

In a high-quality relationship, trust runs deeper. You feel comfortable about disclosing difficulties and dilemmas without worrying about appearing weak or indecisive. The other person respects the fact that you are inviting them to advise you.

*In a high-quality relationship, you feel confident to disclose difficulties and dilemmas, and you are aware of what is implicit in your ask.*

But at the same time, boundaries are understood. They don't probe more than you are ready for. You don't push them too far, and they know that you understand and respect their interests. In the three chapters about the Personal Boardroom roles (Chapters 6 to 8) we talk about what is implicit in the ask for each role. For example, a Connector is allowing you to benefit from their reputation, by making an introduction for you. If you disappoint, it reflects badly on them. When asking someone to be a Connector, you are aware of this implicit liability for them.

Both of you feel able to be honest about your time commitments, and to say no for whatever reason; but when each of you says yes, you mean it.

# Deep, strong, shallow and distant ties

As you settle on the right people, there is one final element to consider, as presented in Table 2.

Table 2: Deep, strong, shallow and distant ties

|  | Your relationship is **distant.** | Your relationship is **close and trusting.** |
|---|---|---|
| You interact **frequently** (monthly or more often). | Shallow ties | Deep ties |
| You interact **infrequently** (less than monthly). | Distant ties | Strong ties |

Table 2 shows four types of relationship, defined by whether the relationship is close and trusting, or distant; and whether you interact frequently or infrequently. By trusting, we mean a deep level of trust in which you can be open about difficulties. People you see infrequently are more likely to be weak ties. (For more on weak ties refer to the beginning of this chapter.)

- A **deep** relationship is close, trusting, and frequent. These are built with very supportive, close-knit people who are either very familiar with you and your work, or close family and friends.

- A **strong** relationship is close and trusting but not frequent. These are relationships that have built up over time through shared experiences and good times together, but you don't interact frequently at the moment. Nonetheless, because of the strong bond between you, you can count on that person's support and willingness to help. The benefit of a strong relationship is that, because you don't see each other often, the person is more likely to bring the novelty and value associated with weak ties.

- A **distant** relationship is not especially close or deeply trusting, and you only see each other infrequently. Distant relationships—because they are almost certainly weak ties— have a huge potential value to connect you with new people and ideas.

- A **shallow** relationship is frequent, but not close or trusting. These are probably colleagues or people you do business with. These could be emerging relationships, which are becoming closer as you get to know each other. But they could also be inherited relationships, with colleagues you do not get on with, or do not trust.

Consider which category each of your Personal Boardroom relationships falls into. We think that strong ties are the most valuable, because they combine intimacy and trust with an outside perspective. Deep ties are also valuable, because their high frequency of contact will bring familiarity and good insights into how you do your job on a daily basis. We encourage distant ties too, for their ability to connect you to different worlds, but not in isolation. We worry about a Personal Boardroom that is full of shallow ties, unless some of these relationships are in the process of becoming deep ties as trust increases.

*Strong ties are the most valuable because they combine an outside perspective with high levels of trust.*

Put each of your Personal Boardroom members into one of these four categories. Then ask yourself the following:

- **Are the majority of relationships deep?** If so, you are able to draw on a powerful levels of support from a close-knit group of people who know you well. However, watch out for groupthink—see the next point.

- **How many of your deep ties know each other,** and interact regularly with each other? If the majority are immersed in a single grouping (such as an executive team) you are at risk of reinforcing each other's ideas, and of groupthink. Could you replace some of these with distant or strong ties?
- **Do you have at least some infrequent relationships** (either distant or strong) to bring novelty and a different way of seeing the world?
- **Reflect on your distant relationships.** They are valuable because of their links to a different world. But would it help to invest in these relationships to make them closer and more trusting? How would you benefit if they became strong relationships?
- **Where are the shallow relationships heading?** If they are emerging, that is a good sign. Invest in the relationship to get to know these people better and to build trust. If they are stagnant or declining, consider whether these people should be in your Personal Boardroom.

You might also think about whether each role is filled by at least one person who is a strong or a deep tie. Since levels of trust are high, these are high-quality relationships. They will be better set up for effective conversations that deliver the role benefits, as you'll see in the next chapter.

# Summary of Chapter 4

Twelve is the optimum number of Personal Boardroom members to deliver all the role benefits without investing huge amounts of time.

When generating a long-list of possible Personal Boardroom members, try to stretch for unlikely possibilities. Doing so may bring some useful ideas.

When narrowing down your long-list, there are four things to consider:

1.    **Baseline rules:** Each person knows you and your work, you trust them (in the role) and your relationship is current or emerging

2.    **It has diversity:** Your Personal Boardroom is made up of people from a variety of backgrounds and contexts with different levels of familiarity with you

3.    **You have a high-quality relationship:** You energise each other, momentum is sustained and boundaries are respected.

4.    **You have one strong or deep tie in each role, and some distant ties.** Any shallow ties are on the way to becoming deeper.

# 5 Have the conversations

*One of the greatest pleasures in life is conversation.*

Sydney Smith, English humorist and cleric[28]

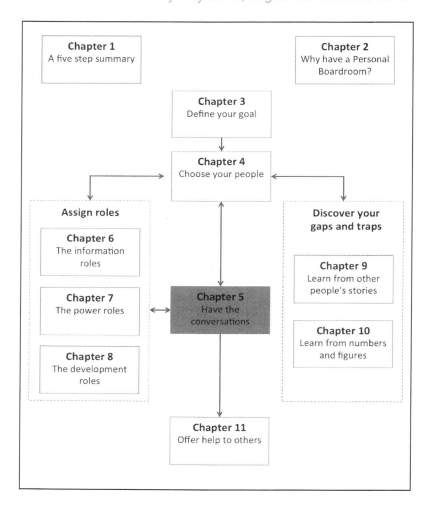

You could read up to this point in the book with the impression that the Personal Boardroom is a nice concept that might, in principle, be useful. But until you have purposeful conversations with your Personal Boardroom members with specific roles in mind, it is still only that: a nice concept. This chapter is about making it real in practice.

In this chapter, we consider how to recruit people into your Personal Boardroom, making a distinction between strategies for people who are already actively supporting you, and those who are not yet doing so.

We address the question of how transparent to be when you first make contact: will you tell people that you'd them like to be a member of your Personal Boardroom, or will you make purposeful requests without revealing the structure you are drawing on? Both approaches are appropriate, and you may opt for different approaches for different members.

People vary in their attitudes toward asking and giving, and we talk about the implications of that. We also suggest ways to get the most value from the conversation.

## Recruiting people into your Personal Boardroom

If you have read Chapter 4 you will now have a list of members, or possible members, of your Personal Boardroom. But you might have been wondering, while reading Chapter 4, whether some of them would actually agree to help you. As yet, they may have no clue that you want to ask them for something. They might be delighted to help, but perhaps you fear that some—especially the distant people—will be surprised or confused by a request, or unwilling to do what you ask.

People will have different motivations for helping you, and it is very useful to anticipate their motivation before you ask. An analogy from charity fundraising is helpful here. Think about the last time you raised money for a charitable cause; for example, doing a sponsored activity like running a marathon.

You approached people and asked them to part with their cash to support you. Why did they agree to give you money? There were probably three sources of motivation:

- **The cause**: They thought the charity you were raising money for was doing valuable and important work, and they wanted to support it.
- **The challenge**: They were impressed at the physical feat you were taking on, and wanted to support you in that endeavour. The fact that you were willing to tackle this difficult thing was the driving factor for their giving.
- **You**: They gave money because it was you who asked. They would have donated irrespective of the cause or the challenge. They knew this was something important to you, and that was enough.

The same set of motivations can be applied to someone's reason for agreeing to be part of your Personal Boardroom. (We talk later in this chapter about whether you explicitly ask them to join your Personal Boardroom, or whether you ask for help without mentioning the words 'Personal Boardroom'.)

Some people will be happy to help because it's **you** who is asking. That might be because they rate you and your work, they like you, or they have known you for years. If they supported you in the past, as a former boss, mentor or colleague, they may expect to do so again. They might help because you are a friend of someone they know. Whatever the reason, they have a straightforward desire to help you succeed, in whatever way they can.

*There are three sources of motivation to give help: the cause, the challenge and the fact that it's you asking.*

Other people will relate to the **challenge** you have set yourself. Let's say you've taken on a very senior leadership role, or a very demanding board-level position, or are setting up a new venture. People who have been there themselves, or have seen others go through it, will know how hard it is. Their willingness to help will come from wanting to pass on their own wisdom, so that you avoid the mistakes they made and benefit from their recipes for success.

Another group of people will be motivated by your challenge because your success will benefit them. For example, a boss supports your promotion case because it demonstrates her good leadership, and reflects well on her team. A colleague backs your plan for a challenging business restructuring because his organisation will benefit.

Lastly, some people will be motivated by the **cause** or the purpose you create. They see *why* what you are doing is important. They are excited by your vision and want to be part of making that happen. It could be that, like the group mentioned above, your success means they stand to benefit, but that is not the primary motivation for helping you. They see a bigger picture—whether that's a better-run business, the growth of an exciting new business model, improved products for consumers, better services for end-users, a happier population, or a greener society.

In the next sections, we delve into some detail about how to make the approach. As you read on, bear in mind the differing reasons your Boardroom members are likely to have for helping you. Try to speak to those motivations as you frame your requests.

## Planning the approach

At some point you are going to bite the bullet and have your first Personal Boardroom conversation. Before you do that, there are some things to decide.

Look at the list of people in your Personal Boardroom. Of the people on that list:

- Who is already actively supporting you and your career?
- Who is not yet actively supporting you and your career?

### People already supporting you and your career

Your first decision, for those actively supporting you, is whether you will formalise a request. This group might include your boss, other senior managers, a mentor, a coach, a former boss, or anyone else who sees it as beneficial to support your career.

For people in this group, consider which of the 12 Personal Boardroom roles each of them is already playing. (If you have not yet done so, read through the twelve role descriptions. They are summarised in Chapter 1; Step 3.) Are there any new roles you would like them to play?

Do you want to formalise their involvement—by talking to them about individual roles or a specific task or challenge—or will it work best to say nothing and carry on as you are? You might have reasons for carrying on as you are, including a large power distance between you, or your preference to keep your Personal Boardroom private, as we discuss further below.

*Formalising the involvement of people who are already helping you makes their help more targeted, and is a good way of showing your appreciation.*

However, formalising the involvement can be valuable for the following reasons:

- Having a conversation about your Personal Boardroom goal (whether this is personal and career-related, or business related) will make them more informed and better able to provide targeted help.
- Having a conversation about the roles they currently play for you is a lovely way of recognising what they do, and making them feel appreciated.
- Talking about a new role you want someone to play is a constructive way of inviting specific help
- If someone plays a lot of roles then it can be very useful to talk about how to structure one-on-one conversations to give space for each role when appropriate, and to make the most of the range of difference resources they provide.

If you decide to formalise their involvement, it may be helpful to introduce the concept of a Personal Boardroom first. We provide further guidance in the section on making the first contact below.

## People not yet supporting you and your career

We often find that our Personal Boardroom diagnostic tool fires up ideas about who to get back in contact with; new thoughts about people who could be useful in a variety of ways; and a dawning recognition of role gaps, and people who could fill them.

So we hope that at some point you will extend a Personal Boardroom invitation to people outside the list of usual suspects. This wider group of people (which might include suppliers, customers, peers, direct reports or friends) may not be expecting such a request from you, and may well be baffled by an outright request to be a member of their Personal Boardroom.

So your next decision is how to make an initial request of these people in a way that maximises the chance of a *yes* and a fruitful conversation to follow. The following two sections, on deciding the conversation strategy and making the approach, help you think through the more delicate aspects of how to approach them.

## What is your conversation strategy?

How open are you willing to be with members of your Personal Boardroom about the fact that they have been chosen? You have two decisions to make:

1.  Will you be open about the concept of a Personal Boardroom and let your members know that you have chosen them to be in it? And will that be with everyone, or with only some members?
2.  If you are open, will you have one-on-one conversations, or a group conversation with all members at once?

There is no right answer; you may have a strong personal preference, and the decision also depends on your Personal Boardroom goal, as we illustrate below.

The **Individual** conversation strategy is where you have one-on-one conversations with Personal Boardroom members, but you do not bring them all together. Within this strategy you can be private or open. If your choose a private approach, you don't let people know they are in your Personal Boardroom. In an open approach, you do.

> *You do not have to tell people you have chosen them for your Personal Boardroom. You can simply ask for their help. That is called a private approach.*

To illustrate this, let's say you want the people in your Personal Boardroom to help you be as effective as you can be as a leader.

You have included direct reports in your Boardroom, as well as your boss, your dotted-line boss, and some of the people who report to these two people. Telling people that they are in your Boardroom would be especially awkward with your direct reports, who are there as Improvers and Influencers, as you prefer a fairly formal relationship as their boss. So you choose an **Individual** and **Private** strategy.

*An individual strategy means you approach one person at a time. You do not invite group conversations.*

Or imagine that you've chosen a task-specific goal, which is to be promoted to vice president by the end of the year. In your Boardroom you have identified two people who can act as Sponsor and Influencer in support of your promotion. With them, you are open about your goal of promotion. Two of your peers are also in your Personal Boardroom as Challengers, Improvers and Navigators. They are there because their feedback and know-how makes you better at the day-to-day aspects of your job. There is no reason to share with them that you are aiming for promotion, and indeed you are actually in competition with one of them. So you choose a **Individual** and **Private/Open** strategy. You let some, but not all, of your members know they are in your Personal Boardroom.

There are times when it can be helpful to bring everyone together as a group. Imagine you have taken up a new position as CEO of a private equity-backed company that is about to go through an IPO. Your time at the moment is consumed with investment bankers and private equity investors. People know this a big step for you, and that there are few people inside the company with relevant experience. Your Personal Boardroom is a group of people you trust—most of them outside the company—who have experience of dealing with major corporate transactions. You choose a **Group** Conversation strategy, inviting them as a group to support you through this challenge.

*In a group conversation, your Personal Boardroom members can pool ideas and build on each other's insights.*

One entrepreneur we know began with an individual strategy, but as his ideas were rapidly developing, he began to feel that his one-on-one updates were very time-consuming. To gain even one new useful connection, challenge, or piece of advice required him to spend time updating each Personal Boardroom member on what was going on. He explored the idea of using a private Google+ circle, so that he could post updates whenever a new development happened, and his Personal Boardroom could contribute in an ongoing way rather than waiting until he picked up the phone. Eventually, he issued an invitation to the whole group to join him in person for a product development workshop.

## Deciding which strategy is right for you

Some things to bear in mind when deciding on your conversation strategy are:

- Think about the goal you identified for your Personal Boardroom. How useful and how appropriate is it that everyone knows that this is your goal?
- If people knew they were in your Personal Boardroom, would they be flattered? Would it increase their motivation to help you? Would it encourage high-quality relationships? Would it make it easier to acknowledge what is implied by your requests for help?
- How damaging would it be if someone close to you found out they were not included?
- Is there benefit in people knowing who else is in your Personal Boardroom? Would they work more effectively together if they knew they had a shared purpose to support you?
- How valuable would it be to have everyone share their own advice, and to hear the advice of others?

- Would it be more efficient for you to pursue a Group strategy, so that you'd spend less time updating people?
- If you are open about the goal of your Personal Boardroom and your intended results, will people think badly of you if you don't achieve it as quickly or effectively as you had hoped?

## Making the first contact

Three are three different ways of making the first contact:

The first is a **membership-based approach**. You ask someone to become one member of a team that will contribute to your success. Specific role requests may follow, but you begin with an invitation to consider themselves as members of your Personal Boardroom. You describe the terms of reference: what the Personal Boardroom is for, and how you propose to interact with its members.

Your first contact might go something like this:

---

I have been thinking recently about … [Insert here the purpose you want to achieve] … and how to achieve that. I would like to draw around me a small group of people I trust to help me with that goal. I have started referring to that group of people as my Personal Boardroom.

I'd like to invite you to be a member of my Personal Boardroom, if you are willing. I'm hoping that you and eleven others [you could mention some of them if known to the person your are talking to] will agree to be part of this with me.

I'm wondering if you would consider playing this specific role / two specific roles / three specific roles, *etc.* which is/are …

---

[Now list each role in turn, with a brief explanation of the role and how it relates to your goal or purpose.]

You would be ideal/absolutely perfect as a/n ... [insert role name] because ... [Explain why.]

Because you are busy, I want to be very clear about what this entails for you. [Explain what you want the person to do, so that the role is bounded in time and scope. If you are inviting people into a Group Conversation, explain how that will work, giving timing and details of how the communication will take place.]

The second is a **task-based approach**. You introduce a task or challenge and ask someone to consider helping with that. Specific role requests follow, but you begin with an explanation of the task itself. You outline a timeframe, and explain what a good result would look like.

Your first contact might go something like this:

I have been thinking recently about ... [Insert here the goal you want to achieve.]

Ideally, I would like to be able to achieve ... [List the results you hope for with a timeframe.]

I'm wondering if you would consider helping me achieve this in the following ways ...

[Describe what you want the person to do, using the role you have in mind as a guide. Explain why the person is ideal for that role.]

> Because you are busy, I want to be very clear about what this entails for you. [Explain what you want them to do, including a timeframe so that the role is bounded in time and scope. If you are inviting people into a Group Conversation, explain how that will work, giving timing and details of how the communication will take place.]

The third is a **role-based approach**. You use the terminology of roles to make a specific request for help. In the three following chapters on roles we give suggestions for how to start a conversation with someone for each role. Here is one example of how to start a conversation with a Navigator:

> Within the next [X months or years] I would very much like to achieve
>
> ... [Insert your Personal Boardroom goal here.]
>
> If I am to be successful, I really need to understand more about ...
>
> [what people will be looking for, who is likely to support or oppose that idea, who I'm likely to be in competition with, what people are currently worrying about or hoping for, *etc.*]
>
> I know that you are much closer to all of this than I am because of your ... [List reasons why they are useful as a Navigator.]
>
> Would you mind spending some time with me so that I can understand this a little better? What are all the things I should know about this?

Whichever approach you choose, being open and straightforward about your intent is the best approach. It will really help if you can provide the following:

- Clarity about the **purpose of the conversation**. Time is the most precious commodity for busy executives, so people need to understand why you want their time.

- A signal that you **understand and respect** their position or interests—especially if you are asking for someone to favour you over someone else, such as other candidates for a position, or other suppliers. All of the roles carry with them implicit demands or expectations, and it may be helpful to show that you recognise these.
- An appreciation of **boundaries**. More than anything, people get spooked by open-ended requests. (Will you be my mentor? is an example of an open-ended request.) From the beginning, if you can demonstrate that your request is limited in time or in scope, people will respect you for that, and their decision about whether they can help will be more informed.

One client of ours, Dan, struggled with how to approach a senior Expert whose knowledge of strategic marketing could help him shape a vision for the marketing of his organisation. He was hesitant about imposing on his intended Expert. It was only when he reflected on his own relationship as a mentor that the right approach became clear. Dan works in an organisation that helps people from corporate backgrounds pursue new careers in social entrepreneurship. He is often asked by graduates of his programme to be their mentor, because of his own experience of the same transition. But there was one only person, Michael, whom he agreed to take on. Michael was very clear about what mentoring him would involve. He laid out the terms—how many chats, over how many months. Dan said:

*'He made it easy for me to decide because I could see what I was getting into. He knew that my time was probably the thing I was most concerned about.'*

If you have decided to follow a Group Conversation strategy, your intention is to invite everyone into a group dialogue. Before you do so, an individual invitation to each person along the lines of the above is all the more important. Give people the courtesy of having the chance to consider whether they want to be part of the group exchange and to opt out if they so choose.

## Different orientations toward asking and giving

When approaching someone to ask for help, which of the following is uppermost in your mind?

- What you can offer them?
- What they owe you?
- What you owe them?

How you react to the questions above reflects your personal style. Building on an extensive body of academic research, Wharton Professor Adam Grant makes a distinction between three types of people: givers, takers and matchers.[29]

If you are a **giver**, you are probably not interested in whether someone owes you anything, because your primary inclination is to help others without expecting or even thinking about a return. As a **matcher**, you would be acutely aware of what you owe. You might, for example, refrain from asking for something because you have already made several requests, and you have not (yet) been able to offer anything back. As a **taker** you find it natural to ask for help without worrying about the balance of reciprocity.

Reflect on your own reciprocity style. (Adam Grant's online resources can help you do this.)[30] If you are a taker, it will feel natural to approach your Personal Boardroom members for help. Be aware of the cautions in Grant's book. Takers tend to burn their boats if they make too many requests for help, or are seen as exploitative—especially by matchers, who are keeping score. It can be harder for takers to rekindle dormant ties for this reason.

*People vary in their orientations towards reciprocity. Reflect on whether you are a taker, a giver or a matcher. Do the same for the people you are asking for help.*

If you are a giver, people might will be surprised to hear from you, as they don't know you as someone who asks; but—especially if they are matchers—they will be pleased to be able to repay some of the good deeds you have done for them.

If you are a matcher—and most of us in a professional capacity are matchers according to Grant—then use the Personal Boardroom as an opportunity to give as well as to take. You will be drawing down favours and making requests of your Boardroom members. You might feel in deficit; but by thinking about paying it forward, as we discuss in Chapter 11, you can tilt the balance of reciprocity back the other way.

Also think about the orientation of the person you are approaching. If they are a matcher, they might be thinking about what you have done for them lately. Consider what you can offer in return. If they are a taker, they are most likely to help if they see something to gain, so it might be useful to explain how your success would reflect on them. If you are approaching a giver, reflect on whether you might be contributing to an overload of requests, and take responsibility for making sure they can opt out or withdraw without feeling compromised.

## Making the most of the conversation

Some of the Boardroom roles require an action by your Boardroom member. This is especially true of the power roles. You want an Influencer to use their skills of persuasion the next time they are in a room with a critical stakeholder. You want an Unlocker to approve a purchase or change a budget line. You want a Sponsor to talk eloquently about how you exceeded expectations last quarter. You want a Connector to fire off an email, or make the phone call that will result in a valued introduction.

The other roles are primarily about talking. A Customer Voice tells you about the market for your new product line. A Navigator chats about who she has seen at conferences recently. An Anchor reminds you about a commitment at the weekend. Some roles, like Inspirer, Challenger or Expert might forward useful documents, or comment on a draft email.

*The primary value of Personal Boardroom membership*
*comes from effective conversations.*

We contend that the value in all of the roles comes from effective conversations. Being able to tap into the potential value of your Personal Boardroom members means doing more listening than talking. Of course, to set up the conversation you need to be clear about what you want and how they can help, and you may need to spend time talking to paint a picture of what is going on. Ultimately, though, you will gain more by giving the other person space to talk.

If you can bear two principles in mind, you are more likely to benefit from the conversation:

## Listen first

We talk throughout this book about asking for help. For all of the roles, that requires you to do one thing very well: to listen. If you can be a good listener, your Boardroom will be more valuable. Whether it's asking a Nerve-Giver to help you carry through on a tough decision, or a Navigator to explain the CEO's current preoccupations, you need to give your Boardroom members space to be heard. Even if you are asking an Unlocker to stump up some cash, or an Influencer to have a word with a resistant stakeholder, it will help enormously if you listen to what they have to say, and understand how they see the world.

> *Especially when you are asking for something,*
> *it is important to listen first.*

So as you enter into any conversation, you might like to remember the RASA acronym. This comes from a TED talk by Julian Treasure, who has made a career out of studying listening.[31]

- **Receive** – by paying attention to what the person is saying.
- **Appreciate** – Show that you are interested and engaged by nodding, following up, ignoring distractions, resisting the temptation to disagree.
- **Summarise** – Show that you have understood. 'So' is a very important word in listening.
- **Ask** – in way that builds on what you've heard.

## Stay with the question

The last element in the RASA acronym is Ask. Questions are a powerful way of inviting solutions. Our brains are wired to answer questions. Rather than saying to a Navigator 'I need a good digital marketing agency', the question 'How might I choose the best digital marketing agency?' will prompt your Navigator to provide answers that will develop and extend your knowledge.

Our natural tendency when confronted with a question or a puzzle is to see the problem, choose a solution—most likely the first one that comes to mind—and then say or do something. If that applies to you, it almost certainly applies to the person you are talking to. They suggest an answer like 'You should talk to Bob or Jan; they had a great experience with a digital marketing agency.' At that point, it is tempting to move away from the question. You start talking about the detail of what Bob or Jan did with a digital marketing agency, and before you know it you are committed to that course of action.

*When seeking information or solutions, ask an open question that encourages a list of answers.*

So it is better if you can ask an open question that encourages a list of answers. For example, you could ask 'What are all the things I need to think about when choosing a digital marketing agency?' Talking with Bob or Jan might be one answer, but another might be to look up recent agency awards, or to talk to some reference clients. Your request for multiple suggestions allows you to return to the question and ask 'What else could I do?' At the end of the conversation, you can revisit your list and evaluate which is the best suggestion.

These simple principles—listening first and staying with the question—will provide the foundation for a conversation in which your Personal Boardroom members feel heard, respected and valued, and in which you are open to their ideas. That kind of conversation should be energising for both you and the other person.

## Reflecting on the conversation

Time for reflection gets squeezed out of the day-to-day routine. But Personal Boardroom conversations should be up there with the most strategic, revealing and challenging discussions you have each day. They are personal and intimate conversations that will shape your future as well as your present. So it is well worth finding time to reflect on what you heard, what you learned, and what that means.

You will be exposed to a range of diverse viewpoints and perspectives. You will hear conflicting opinions. A typical corporate board meeting covers an array of subjects, and people around the table will chip in where they have something valuable to add. In the same way, your Personal Boardroom will channel a large volume of information towards you across a range of subject matter. They will expect you to take action and seize opportunities they create for you, and to see that you delivered. They will press you on your core purpose, and insist on making you accountable. Some of the feedback and challenges will be difficult to hear.

> *See yourself as the chair of your Personal Boardroom. It is your job to lead and shape the conversations.*

See yourself as the chair of your Personal Boardroom. You need to manage the flow of advice and assistance: inviting it when needed; using it where it is relevant and timely to do so; and being able to put it aside when it is not. This is your Personal Boardroom and you need to lead it and shape the conversations.

You also need to be willing to reconfigure it. Designing a Personal Boardroom is an iterative process involving a series of build-test-learn loops. In the **build phase**, you identify a purpose for your Boardroom, choose people, and assign roles. In the **test phase** you try out conversations with them. In the **learn phase** you reflect on the information they gave you, their willingness to help, and whether they can deliver what you want.

To enable that, reflection is very valuable. After a conversation with a Personal Boardroom member, ask yourself:

- What went well and what didn't go well?
- What was planned or expected, and what was unplanned or unexpected?

Combining these two dimensions together:

- **Things that you planned and which went well** were clearly a success. For example you asked someone for specific help and they agreed. Remember how they felt and what you said or did. This might be a tactic you could use again the next time you talk to this person, or someone else.
- **Things that were unplanned but went well** are an added bonus. For example, the conversation led into areas you did not anticipate, but with good results. Reflect on whether there was something you said or did that helped the conversation take a positive course. Could you do so again in another situation? If so, plan for this the next time.
- **Things that you planned but went badly** could be because you misjudged a person or a situation. Reflect on whether it was something to do with you, or the other person, or some aspect of the place and time, or your method of approach. If it was you, could you be more effective next time? Could you phrase things differently or make a different request? If it was the setting or timing, make a note to avoid that the next time if you can.
- The same applies to **things that you didn't plan, that went badly**. Was it you, the other person, or the setting? What could you take away from this for the next conversation?

Reflecting in this way may lead to new thoughts about what you want your Personal Boardroom to help with, new ideas for Boardroom members, and new thoughts on roles. Be willing to respond to the insights that these conversations bring.

There may well be action to take as a consequence of the conversation—for you and for your Personal Boardroom. As we explored in Chapter 4, it's important that both of you deliver on your promises and commitments if you are to benefit from a high-quality relationship.

## Summary of Chapter 5

There are three sources of motivation to give help: the cause, the challenge and the fact that it's **you** asking.

Conversations can be individual (one-on-one), or with a group; and private (you don't reveal that you've chosen someone for your Personal Boardroom), or open.

There are three ways of making the first contact: membership-based, task-based, and role-based.

People vary in their orientations to reciprocity. There are givers, matchers and takers. Bear your orientation in mind, and that of the person you are approaching.

To get the most of the conversation, listen first and stay with the question.

To reflect on the conversation think about two elements: what went/didn't go well? and what was planned/unplanned?

# 6 The information roles

*Knowledge is of two kinds. We know a subject ourselves, or we know where we can find information upon it.*

Samuel Johnson, writer and lexicographer[32]

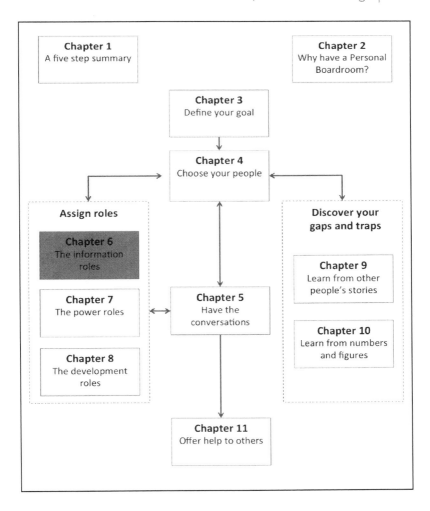

In this chapter we examine the four Information roles in your Personal Boardroom. Information roles provide access to knowledge, insights, perspectives and ideas you would not otherwise have. Your Customer Voices and your Navigators give you a window into worlds that are different from yours, and landscapes you are not familiar with. You cannot know everything, so your Experts step in for things you know little about, and extend and deepen your knowledge where it is already strong. Your Inspirers bring new and surprising perspectives.

For each, we consider the primary job associated with this role, and what kind of person you might look to. We give examples that might stimulate ideas about who could fill a role. In each case, we make suggestions about how to start a conversation with the role in mind.

*Each role carries with it some expectations and assumptions about how you and the other person will act. Being aware of this is vital for high-quality relationships.*

We also explore what is implicit when you ask someone to take on each role. Each carries with it some expectations and assumptions about how you and the other person will act. These are not always made explicit when we make requests. However, being aware of them, and where necessary being open about them, is vital if you are to have high-quality relationships with the members of your Personal Boardroom.

## Customer Voice

We call this role the Customer Voice, and illustrate it with a target, because this role gives you a deep insight into the minds of people you are ultimately here to serve. Your customers are the people who, by purchasing your product or using your service, determine whether you and your team will be successful. That might be by spending more on your company's products or services, being more productive as employees, or channelling more investment in your direction. They may be external to your company, or internal.

*Your Customer Voice is a specific person within your customer base who has a perspective on how your product or service, or the work of your team, is perceived.*

By listening to your Customer Voice, you gain a better understanding of the expectations and mindsets of your customers: how they feel, what they really value, what they get perplexed about, *etc*. Your Customer Voice helps you see where the opportunities are to do things better, or to do better things.

The term 'Customer Voice' is relatively flexible here. You might also want to think about the voices of your investors, employees, suppliers, or service-users.

## Example: Customer Voice

Richard, a corporate lawyer in a top London firm described the close relationship he has with a General Counsel in a FTSE 100-listed firm. The client organisation has several law firms on its panel of advisers. However, this GC likes and trusts Richard and his firm on the basis of high-quality work on past transactions. When the CFO moved on, Richard was given the heads-up and invited to meet the new CFO, whose endorsement would determine whether Richard's firm won pitches for business in the future. This example shows how Customer Voices can provide useful insights into networks of influence inside client organisations.

## How to start a conversation with a Customer Voice

My team are interested in/thinking of ...

[launching a new version of brand Y; targeting a new customer base; entering a new market; revisiting the branding around product X; changing the way we do something; pitching to company Z, etc.]

Can you tell me how this product/service/idea/change would be perceived by people like you if we were to do this?

What are all the things you would like to see in a product or service like this?

### What is implicit in the ask?

You're asking a Customer Voice to give a different perspective from your own. Try not to jump to your defence if they start to be critical—you want a frank opinion after all.

Think carefully about how much information they need from you to do their job well. Can you make it easy for them to provide you with valuable insights, without taking up too much of their time? Most customers are happy about product or service improvements, so you can rely on their goodwill if what you are proposing is in their interest.

But don't be devious. You might be tempted to fish for information about who their key decision-makers are, or what the budget is, or who else has their business now. These are classic sales techniques and have their place, but if this person is in your Personal Boardroom, a trust-based relationship is what you are after. Do not leave them feeling used or compromised.

### Ask yourself:

•   Are the people you've chosen as Customer Voices representative of your immediate customers, clients or stakeholders?

- Are the end-users of your products or services represented?
- If your most important customers are in a particular age, gender or ethnic group, is your Customer Voice able to represent this group?
- Do they bring a very different perspective from what you currently know? If you have already done a lot of business with these people, is their perspective fresh enough?
- Who can help you understand markets you are not yet in, or opportunities that you are not currently pursuing as a business?

## Expert

 We call this role the Expert, and illustrate it with a book, because this role gives you access to deep expertise that you do not have, or very specific experience relevant to the challenge you are facing. That might be knowledge of an industry sector, or a cultural perspective on another country; or it might be advice drawn from someone's technical or professional knowledge.

*Your Experts are the people who fill the gaps in your knowledge much more quickly than you could do yourself.*

You rely on your Experts' good judgment, which is honed by experience. By listening to them, you will save time and make better decisions.

### Example: Expert

Diana, country manager of a corporate subsidiary, inherited a team when she moved from New York to take up a role as the German country manager. The company as a whole was highly demanding in terms of what it expected its executive teams to deliver, and Diana worried that she would not hit her targets unless she found a way to manage two difficult individuals out of her team and replace them with people she rated. During her first few months in the new role, Diana's local HR partner, a German national, strongly advised her against taking any disciplinary action, claiming this would take years to implement, and in the meantime would create mistrust and undermine morale.

The local HR partner was doing his job, but Diana felt increasingly frustrated by her team's under-performance. She turned to Jacob, the Danish country manager. Jacob had previously worked in Germany, and had experience of the constraints of the employment law and the works councils system. He helped Diana develop solutions for reorganising the roles of the two difficult people without moving them out of the team. Jacob's expertise helped Diana find constructive ways of working within a different national and legal system.

As another example, Ben Horowitz described the expert advice given to him by Michael Ovitz, about how to handle a negotiation in which IBM and EDS were both interested in acquiring his company, LoudCloud. Time and money were running out, and the deal had to be done quickly. Ovitz was 'the most powerful deal-maker in Hollywood' according to Horowitz.[33] The blunt advice given was to play them against one another, which Horowitz did by telling them both they had to complete the process in eight weeks or withdraw.

As a business leader, being able to call on people with tried and tested experience, like Michael Ovitz, or on the deep knowledge of professionals or technical experts, can be enabling. Experts give a tangible sense of what it possible, and help to navigate barriers and constraints. As founders of a start-up business, friendly advice from an accountant and an IP lawyer has been extremely helpful for us. With external Experts, however, there is a balance to be struck between seeking free advice and paying for services, as we explore further below.

## How to start a conversation with an Expert

I'm currently …

[facing some challenges with X/wondering how to deal with Y/thinking about doing Z].

If I am to be successful, I really need some help with …

[List the advice you want.]

It's particularly complicated/troubling/urgent because …

[List reasons.]

I know that you have a great deal of experience in this area. I'd very much value a little of your time, to talk specifically about …

[Have a list of questions, ideally phrased to invite multiple responses. For example: What are all the things I should be aware of about X? What are all the factors that will affect Y?]

## What is implicit in the ask?

You are asking your Expert to save you time by helping you with something you could do yourself, or to save you money by providing you with advice that you would otherwise have to pay for, or to save your soul by helping you with a difficult situation. Many people, especially people who have learned from experience, are delighted to share what they have learned, and will get pleasure from doing so.

However, there is a fine line with external Experts, especially if your Experts make a living from giving the kind of advice you are seeking. This does not matter so much with one conversation, but if you are to involve them as a Boardroom member on an ongoing basis, how much help do you need?

Where is the point at which they start to feel you are asking too much? Making your request time-limited might help. Another tactic is to ask them to be clear about the point at which they need to start charging you, so you are not surprised by an unexpected invoice for their services.

## Ask yourself:

- What knowledge gaps are you are facing now? What are the most acute knowledge gaps you will face in the next few months? (Think back to the purpose of your Personal Boardroom.)
- Are the people you have chosen as Experts the best people to fill those gaps?
- Are your Experts people who will want, or expect, you to give them some business? Are you in a position to pay for their advice? How can you be clear about the boundaries between free and paid-for advice?
- Who has been in your shoes and would be pleased to share their experience?

## Inspirer

 We call this role the Inspirer, because your Inspirers light up opportunities by making unexpected connections. Your Inspirers might be people who move in different worlds to you, which means they connect you with news, models, theories, practices, gossip and ideas that you would not discover for yourself. Or they could be in your world, but with a very different way of interpreting what they see.

*Inspirers are special because of their energy and passion, and because they push the boundaries of your thinking.*

Either way, there is something special about an Inspirer, and that is the energy and passion with which they communicate. With them, everything seems interesting and exciting because they have a compelling way of talking. Their energy gets your brain buzzing and your creative juices flowing, and forges connections in your mind. Somehow, they make it possible not only to be inspired by new possibilities going on somewhere else, but also to apply those new ideas to things you already know about. They help you push the boundaries of your own thinking.

Note that this definition of an Inspirer is not that of a role model. We are not talking here about a person who inspires you from a distance, like a celebrity you have always admired, or a revered business leader. An Inspirer is someone in your immediate circle who you talk to and bounce ideas around with, and who makes you feel more creative when you're with them.

## Example: Inspirer

Darren, a social entrepreneur, told us about his irregular career path. In the last 15 years he has regularly shifted gear and direction to suit his evolving interests, and many of his career changes have been as a consequence of talking to entrepreneurs. He's drawn towards them—and particularly to social entrepreneurs—because of their passion and drive to develop new ways of doing things. He described one of his Inspirers, Ian, as a polymath: someone who is an expert in lots of different things. Darren has observed how Ian can connect ideas from all these various domains and use this insight gained from combining and synthesising like this to build one business idea after another. Darren told us that he is keen to create his own venture in a couple of years time, and keeping people like Ian in his life sparks his own ideas about what he might do.

## How to start a conversation with an Inspirer

I'm looking for new ways to think about ...

[Add your service, product, or business problem here.]

... and I'd love to hear what that sparks for you. What have you come across recently that I might find useful? Tell me all the ways in which I could take this idea forward.

Alternatively, with an Inspirer, simply ask what they have been thinking about recently, and see where the conversation takes you.

## What is implicit in the ask?

You are asking your Inspirer to bring into your Personal Boardroom a different perspective from your own. Allow them to hold the floor and try not to shape the direction of the conversation too much.

The relationship with an Inspirer is not always an easy one. You might leave a conversation feeling over-stimulated, or frustrated because you didn't cover the subject you wanted. They are not always good listeners because they love talking about what excites them. You may not always be able to frame the conversation or set goals for it. If you do, you risk limiting the possibility for new discoveries.

Think of it as creating conditions for serendipity. You set up the conversation so that you can be fired up by new thinking. It won't always work, but when it does, it will be vital for re-fuelling your capacity for new ideas.

## Ask yourself:

• Where are your Inspirers drawn from? Do they, between them, represent a social or business world that is not the same as your own? Are they doing different things from you, and connected to different people?

- Are your Inspirers people who excite and energise you? Are they distant role models (in which case they don't fit the definition used here) or are they people you interact with—who fire you up?

- Do you conclude conversations with your Inspirers feeling frustrated as well as inspired? How can you manage the conversation to create the conditions in which you might discover new and useful thinking, without feeling frustrated if you don't?

## Navigator

 We call this role the Navigator, and illustrate it with a ship's wheel because this role helps you chart your way through difficult, unpredictable or unknown waters. If organisations were straightforward places, where everyone was frank, rational and open-minded, and where there was a collective vision for where the organisation should go, you would not need Navigators. But many organisations are not like that. People are idiosyncratic, teams have vested interests, colleagues have differing views, positions can become entrenched, and routines get established that can be hard to change. Even if you have a good understanding of how things work in your own organisation, you may need help deciphering how a client or target client organisation works (or an industry regulator, or a government agency).

*Navigators are the people who can tell you how things work, who thinks and does what, and where vested interests lie.*

By listening to a Navigator, you learn things about your company (who are the rising stars? what is top priority for your boss's boss?); or about competitors (which adviser or agency is working for whom?) or about your industry (which company is investing in what market?), that help you do your job better.

Navigators are not necessarily powerful or senior people. Executive assistants often have a very good knowledge of how work really gets done. Navigators might have been in the organisation for a long time, or have a big network. They might be observers or commentators on an industry, like journalists, analysts or people in a trade body or pressure group. But they can also be quiet individuals who are good observers of people, or who have a great memory for names, faces and conversations.

## Examples: Navigator

Khalid, the marketing director of a UK subsidiary of a global Internet brand told us how from time to time he put a call into Aaron, a colleague in the company's headquarters in Silicon Valley. Aaron happens to be someone Khalid recruited into the company a few years earlier, and before that they both worked in marketing for the same bank. Although they work in different continents and do not meet often, they have a shared history and great deal of respect for each other.

Khalid reports to Cynthia, the global VP of Marketing. Cynthia has a reputation as a slightly faddish boss; whatever her latest concern is, everyone has to know about it. Aaron does not work for her directly, but because he sits near her team, he tends to pick up on the latest 'Cynthia' issue. At some point in the call to Aaron, Khalid works in his standard question: *What's Cynthia worrying about at the moment?* Aaron will let him know that Cynthia is worrying about marketing acquisition, or small business sales, *etc.*

At his next meeting or call with Cynthia, Khalid makes sure that marketing acquisition or small business sales—whatever Cynthia is worrying about—is the first thing he mentions: *The UK numbers are looking really good, but to be honest I am slightly worried about marketing acquisition.* By using Aaron as a Navigator, Khalid is able to anticipate and respond to his boss's latest agenda.

Another example comes from Brad, who spent the first decade of his career in an international consulting firm. Just around the time when being promoted to partner was becoming a tangible goal rather than a distant dream, he received a low performance rating. His manager did not think he was partner material. The mentor who was supposed to look after his career had no interest in disagreeing with the manager. This was bitter news, especially as Brad was working all hours and weekends for the firm.

He took matters into his own hands. First, he went to the HR head for his division and insisted on a change of mentor. Next he invited the new mentor, Sue, out to lunch. Before the lunch he compiled a list of the things he thought he needed to do to be promoted. Over lunch, he put the list in front of his new mentor and asked her opinion. Sue worked through the list and picked out six items that she thought would help Brad make partner.

Over the following months Brad resolved not to do anything that was not in the list. He stopped doing client work at weekends, and started focusing his time on doing the things that Sue, as his Navigator, had singled out. Within a year, and without working another weekend, Brad received his promotion.

## How to start a conversation with a Navigator

Within the next [X months or years] I would very much like to achieve ...

[Insert your Personal Boardroom goal here.]

If I am to be successful, I really need to understand more about ...

> [what people will be looking for; who is likely to support or oppose that idea; who I'm likely to be in competition with; what people are currently worrying about or hoping for, *etc.*]
>
> You are much closer to all of this than I am because of your ...
>
> [List reasons why they are useful as a Navigator.]
>
> Would you mind spending some time with me so that I can understand this a little better? What are all the things I should know about this?

## What is implicit in the ask?

You are asking your Navigator to share information that is potentially very useful for you, but you do not want the sharing of it to be compromising to them. Try not to put a Navigator in a position where s/he feels under pressure, or exploited. The information you are asking for might be construed as gossip, or as undermining to others. Some people love sharing gossip because it gives them a sense of power; others see it as disloyal.

Be careful about how you ask, and keep in mind that a direct request for information that is potentially sensitive or personal may upset someone. Trust and mutual respect is really important here, as it is for all Personal Boardroom relationships.

## Ask yourself:

- How complete is your knowledge about what it takes to get the next level in your business? (Think back to the purpose of your Personal Boardroom.)
- Which individuals have agendas that you need to be aware of? Which teams in another part of your company have goals or vested interests that could affect your success?
- How well do you understand the competitor landscape outside your firm?

- Who in your Personal Boardroom is giving you a window into these questions? What can you do for them in return? Will they gain pleasure from being helpful? Can you let them know how their information helped you?

## Summary of Chapter 6

Information roles provide access to knowledge, insights, perspectives and ideas you would not otherwise have.

Each role carries expectations and assumptions about how you and the other person will act. It is important to be aware of these.

Customer voices provide insight into the minds of people you are here to serve, and help you understand markets and business opportunities.

Experts bring deep expertise that you do not have, or very specific experience relevant to the challenge you are facing.

Inspirers bring new ideas and push the boundaries of your thinking; and they do it in a way that fires you with energy and excitement.

Navigators tell you who you need to know, and who does what.

# 7 The power roles

*The most common way people give up their power is by thinking they don't have any.*

Alice Walker[34]

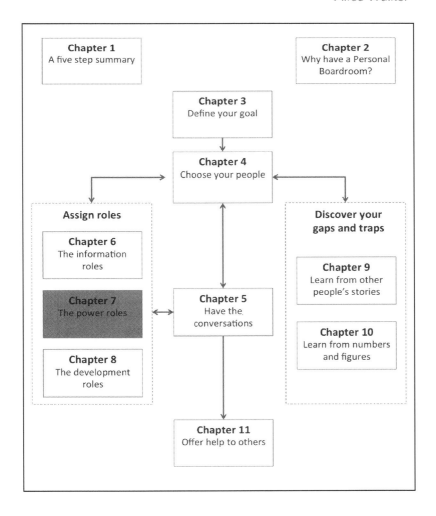

In this chapter we consider the four Power roles in your Personal Boardroom. Power roles allow you to get things done, and reach people and opportunities you would not otherwise be able to access. Your Unlockers provide the resources that are not directly within your control. Your Sponsors and Influencers help secure the success of things you really care about either by endorsing what you are doing or cooperating and building support behind the scenes. Your Connectors are bridges to different social groups, and invite you to benefit from their reputation.

As in the previous chapter, we consider the primary job associated with this role, and what kind of person you might look to. We give examples, offer suggestions about how to start a conversation with the role in mind, and explore what is implicit when you ask someone to take on each role.

## Unlocker

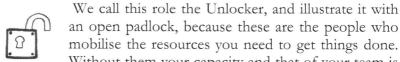 We call this role the Unlocker, and illustrate it with an open padlock, because these are the people who mobilise the resources you need to get things done. Without them your capacity and that of your team is constrained. With their help you have more freedom to manoeuvre. You have more resources or larger budgets. You have people willing to give their time. You can lay hands on physical things like materials, facilities or equipment; or virtual things like datasets, software or processing power. Things happen faster. Decisions are made quicker. Processes are expedited or circumvented.

> *Unlockers provide access to the resources you need to get things done.*

Put another way, your Unlockers are your turbo-chargers. They help you get things done in faster, bigger, better ways.

Unlockers are particularly powerful in accessing resources that you or your team do not have control over. Your Unlocker might be your boss, or a senior person in the organisation, but it could be a peer or someone outside the organisation who is keen to support what you do.

## Example: Unlocker

Cameron was head of the US office of a global advertising agency. The agency served global clients, but organised itself into national units, so all revenues and costs were accounted for on a country-by-country basis. The agency's clients expected to be served by a team drawn from across the world, especially when they were working on a global campaign that was to be rolled out in multiple countries and languages.

To fully staff a campaign for a US motor company, Cameron needed to bring in colleagues from Brazil, Beijing and London and persuade them to relocate for 12 months. There was a fabulous copywriter in the Rio de Janeiro office who the client wanted on the team. Cameron encountered major resistance from the copywriter's boss in the Rio office to the idea of losing him for up to a year. The copywriter was only released after Cameron appealed to the head of the Rio office.

You never know when you are going to need an Unlocker. In this case, Cameron did not have a background with the man who ran the Rio office. Luckily for him, the Rio head was a US national who was keen that the motor company's campaign should succeed, and was prepared to use his rank to make sure the right people were put on the job.

Unlockers can be blockers if they choose not to act in your favour. Ben Horowitz wrote about a client, Frank Johnson (not his real name), who had absolute control over all the servers at EDS, his largest customer representing 90% of revenue at the time. At Frank Johnson's insistence, EDS planned to end a contract with Horowitz's company, Opsware. Johnson claimed their product was 'the biggest goddam piece of shit'. [35]

Through a fortunate disclosure, the Opsware team discovered that Frank liked an inventory product from a company called Tangram, and that the EDS purchasing team were forcing him to switch to an alternative that was free. Horowitz's company went to the lengths of purchasing the Tangram company, and arranging to supply Tangram free with Opsware. This arrangement saved the EDS contract. This is an extreme example, but it forcefully illustrates the need to work Unlockers around to your side.

## How to start a conversation with an Unlocker

I'm currently starting to plan for ...

[Describe your goal.]

This is an exciting project because ...

[State a vision of what this will achieve.]

To be successful we will need ...

[Summarise all the requirements—facilities, budget, resource, equipment, *etc.*—not just those you want from the Unlocker.]

I'm pleased to say that we have already secured ...

[Explain what has already been committed by others, or by your team.]

Would you be willing and able to provide the following to help make this happen?

[Be specific about what you need.]

## What is implicit in the ask?

You are asking your Unlocker to look favourably on your project or agenda. If your Unlocker is your boss, you hopefully have a strong overlap of interests. Your success should reflect well on your boss.

However, that does not always make it easy for the Unlocker. Consider whether your gain is someone else's loss. Are the resources you want shareable? Your boss may be in a difficult position if seen to favour you over someone else.

If the Unlocker works in another team or outside the business, you may have to work hard to demonstrate the benefit to them, as Ben Horowitz had to do for Frank Johnson.

## Ask yourself:

- Where is the upside for your Unlockers in helping you? How can you make this a win-win? What are his/her interests, and is there something you can offer that's valuable in return?
- How can you make it easier for the Unlocker to do what you're asking? What assurances will help?
- Can the resources you want be shared? If not, who is going to lose out? What is the Unlocker's relationship with that person? Can you do anything to ease that relationship?

# Sponsor

 We call this role the Sponsor, and illustrate it with a thumbs-up because your Sponsor makes a point of publicly endorsing you and your work. Sponsors can be internal: for example, a Sponsor might speak up for the work of your team in a budget-planning process, or endorse you in a performance-calibration session, or on a promotion panel. They can also be external, such as reference clients giving a testimonial about the value of your product or service.

*Sponsors are advocates who look after your interests so that other people—who have control over an outcome that you value—make a decision in your favour.*

People often look within their direct reporting line for Sponsors, and indeed it is important that your boss and your boss's boss speak out for you. But support from people outside your direct reporting line can be more powerful. Endorsements from senior people in other business units or functions, and from clients, suppliers or partners outside the company can make all the difference in promotion decisions, sales pitches, and for the success of all kinds of projects and initiatives.

## Example: Sponsor

Marco spent several years helping HR managers in the European operation of a global company collect and analyse data and metrics on human capital. These data reveal whether employee outcomes such as rates of absenteeism, turnover, retention or engagement are trending in the right direction. Marco's boss liked his work and brought it to the attention of Chris, the global VP of HR operations. Chris was a supporter of greater use of metrics in the company, and agreed that better use of data on human capital would improve business performance.

Chris became a Sponsor for Marco and his team, and started lobbying senior colleagues in the US. Among them was Louise, global head of HR, who had a seat on the executive board. Louise was not naturally inclined toward analytical or data-driven ways of operating, but as she trusted and respected Chris, she arranged for him to advocate for greater use of human-capital data at a meeting of the executive board. Marco's Sponsor was now speaking out for him at the highest level. As a consequence, Marco was given a new role, responsible for rolling out human capital measurement into the US operation.

In the first months of Marco's new role, the organisation went through some changes and Chris announced he was taking early retirement. Marco was now more senior, with more resources, and had a remit from the board, but his main Sponsor was gone. He now looked to Louise as his main Sponsor, but he had to work much harder to make sure that Louise, who is less ardent about his work than Chris was, was still acting on his behalf.

Another example of a Sponsor was give to us by Anne, a litigation lawyer in a London law firm. As a large private-practice firm, its bread and butter is large financial transactions, and most of this business is won by the corporate and finance lawyers. They are supported by specialist lawyers like Anne, who deal with disputes, tax, and intellectual property. Anne relied for about half of her work on her colleagues inside the firm, and the other half came from barristers, forensic accountants and client referrals.

Anne told us about a female general counsel (GC) in one of the firm's large clients. Anne had been involved in several deals for the GC's company. This woman rated Anne and her work, and she would go out of her way to tell Anne's colleagues—the senior and most powerful lawyers in her firm—how good she was. The GC acted as a Sponsor, helping Anne to build her reputation inside her own firm.

## How to start a conversation with a Sponsor

In the next few months [or some other timeframe] I am aiming to ...

[Mention the thing that the Sponsor can help with.]

I'm aware that any opportunity to ...

> [Mention things that will help your case and that the Sponsor has some influence over: *e.g.* gain visibility with senior colleagues or decision-makers, or make people aware of my and my team's work] ... will be extremely important.
>
> Would you be willing to mention my name if the opportunity comes up? Is there any information you need about me that would help you do that?
>
> And do let me know of any other things I should be doing in the meantime that will make it easier for you?

OR, in the run-up to a promotion decision:

> I am currently working on/hoping for ...
>
> [Mention the thing that the Sponsor can help with—for example, a case for promotion.]
>
> I know that you will have some input into the final decision. I'd like to tell you about what I/we have been doing so that you and your colleagues can make an informed decision. I'm sure other people will be doing the same, so I just want to be sure that you hear from me along with everyone else.

OR, if you want someone to write a reference:

> I am/my team are currently applying for/pitching for business with X.
>
> You are one of the people closest to my/our work, and as you know I/we have recently achieved ...
>
> [Mention reasons why you are worth sponsoring.]
>
> Would you consider endorsing my/our work by ...
>
> [Explain what you want them to do.]

## What is implicit in the ask?

Your Sponsor is putting their reputation on the line for you. In some cases they might have to fight their corner to make sure you are the one given the business, the bonus, the promotion, or the top performance rating. If you screw up, they look bad.

Much has been written about Sponsors and the valuable role they can play, for example in helping women gain visibility. People have said that sponsorship needs to be earned. We agree. You cannot force a Sponsor to be your advocate—they have to believe in you.

There are times—especially where there is competition for a top performance rating or a promotion—when you cannot make an outright request. Otherwise, you risk putting your intended Sponsor in a difficult position. If their opinion about you is a mix of favourable and unfavourable, or if they think someone else has a stronger case, they cannot promise to support you wholeheartedly. So be ready for a no, or a frank response.

But even if you don't ask outright, you can still have someone in mind as your Sponsor. Then provide them with all the evidence they need about you to make their own judgment. Even if you don't help them in this way, you should assume that someone else who is competing for that contract, promotion or endorsement will be doing so.

And if tempted to put someone's name down as a reference, whether in a job application, a case for promotion or a pitch for business, do them the courtesy of asking first; otherwise, you are on the back foot before you have even started.

## Ask yourself:

• What does your Sponsor need to know about you and your achievements to do the job of a Sponsor well?

- Is your relationship with your Sponsor up to date? Are you relying on 'stale' relationships with people who used to know your work, but are out of touch with it now?

- Are you expecting your Sponsor to endorse you over and above other candidates for the same opportunity? What have you done to show that you are as worthy as, or more worthy than, the other candidates?

- Do your Sponsors include people outside your reporting line, such as senior people in other business units or functions, or clients, suppliers and partners outside the company?

## Influencer

 We call this role the Influencer, and illustrate it with a force field, because of the unseen but powerful effect this role has. Unlike a Sponsor who speaks openly on your behalf, an Influencer works behind the scenes. They have quiet words with important people that convey positive opinions about and support of your work. These gatekeepers might be clients you are pitching to, or colleagues who are resisting your change agenda, or senior people who need to know about what you are doing.

> *Influencers are able to be effective because other people respect them.*

Influencers tend to have a good reading of who listens to whom, and what priorities or agendas are important to their colleagues. They are not always senior. Your direct reports and peers can act as Influencers for you when they support your projects and initiatives, and make sure that other people get behind them.

## Example: Influencer

Bill was an M&A Director in a global pharmaceutical company. The new finance director, Michelle, quickly identified him as a key player in her mission to change how finance is perceived in her organisation.

It was partly Bill's cross-functional role that made him an Influencer for Michelle: he knew many people in different parts of the business. But it was also his personality. Unlike a lot of people in the company, Bill was always walking around the office. He seemed to be the one who got people together. In Michelle's first week, he organised drinks so that she could get to know the other directors. Michelle had the sense that if Bill supported her mission, other people would too.

Another example of an Influencer comes from John, a senior clinician who joined a healthcare organisation. He quickly spotted an opportunity to make changes to how patients are prepared for surgical procedures that would save the organisation money. Too many procedures were being postponed or cancelled because pre-surgical checks had not been carried out correctly or on time. By placing the responsibility for these checks with the nursing team, rather than doctors, they could be carried out more systematically at lower cost.

John put forward his proposals to his surgeon colleagues, who were very resistant. They had a financial incentive to retain control of the budgets associated with the pre-surgical checks. They did not trust John, who was perceived to be a disruptive newcomer.

It was only when John met Carol that he was able to win support for his idea. Carol was junior to John, and a member of the nursing team in an organisation where nurses are deemed to be less important than doctors. However, Carol had been in the organisation for a long time and was respected by many of the senior surgeons. She could see that his suggestion for pre-surgical checks would have better outcomes for patients. She took it upon herself to convince the surgeons to support John's idea. Over time, her influence worked and John's idea was accepted.[36]

## How to start a conversation with an Influencer

I'm currently working on ...

[Describe your project or idea.]

... and I think it would be great for the business or our customers because ...

[Describe your vision for why this is important, or explain the benefits.]

What do you think about this idea?

[Give your Influencer a chance to express their own thoughts and opinions so that you understand where they stand.]

This may be enough information for an Influencer. You do not necessarily have to ask outright for their support, and indeed as we note below, they may be more motivated to help if you don't. In the example above, Bill's endorsement of Michelle's mission for finance meant much more because she did not ask for it, than if she had done.

But if you do want to proceed, you could say:

I know people will look to you for an opinion on this. Can I take some time to explain the benefits to you, as I really believe it is the right thing for us to do.

## What is implicit in the ask?

An Influencer uses the power of their respected status in the organisation to support your cause. Their conviction and motivation to help will be greatest when they believe in what you are doing, and are acting on their own accord, rather than because you have appealed to them to do something for you, or pressured them into it. Bear this in mind when you make a request. Do so lightly, in a way that allows them to opt out.

One of the unfortunate aspects of organisational life is that some people wield a negative influence, seeking to undermine or block good ideas, or pushing their own agenda at the expense of others'. Your Influencers can act to dissipate this resistance on your behalf, as the example from John and Carol showed. But bear in mind that their actions—while positive to you—may be seen as negative by others.

Influence is a powerful weapon. Use it for the good of the whole business. Don't ask your Influencer to take sides. Appeal to common interests and a shared vision. Don't be tempted to ask someone to do your dirty work by having difficult conversations or confronting someone, when it would be more honest to have that conversation yourself.

## Ask yourself:

- Are you at risk of putting an Influencer in a difficult position by making a direct request to support you and your agenda over someone else's?
- Do your Influencers understand your goals and objectives, and do they know enough about what you do? How can you help them tell your story in rating reviews and talent sessions, to accurately portray you to others?
- How can you show your Influencer that what you stand for is worth pursuing for everyone, and is in the wider interests of the business?
- Are you deferring responsibility for challenging or difficult conversations to your Influencer? Would it show more integrity, and ultimately lead to a better outcome, if you were to have these conversations yourself?

## Connector

We call this role the Connector, and illustrate it with a figure of one person bringing together two others because this role is the conduit through which to expand your network and get to know people you could not otherwise reach.

Your Connectors are great at what they do, because they get huge satisfaction out of bringing people together and spotting opportunities to bridge gaps. In fact, they relish it so much that they cannot help but introduce people who they feel should know each other. Because they create great value for others through introductions, they tend to accrue a large number of connections themselves—people who appreciate them for the value their bring.

*A Connector sets up introductions in a warm and informative way that makes the new relationship likely to succeed.*

There is a clear difference between a Navigator and a Connector. A Navigator is a great reader of a social interactions, and can tell you who is a good person to know. A Connector will actually make the introduction for you, and will do so with warmth and encouragement in a way that makes both of you want to know each other. That means they do more than a one-line email introduction that says *You two should know other. I'll leave you to it and step out of the way.* A good Connector wants your new relationship to succeed, and will invest time to explain the possibilities to both of you, making sure that you both understand the value that can follow from knowing each other.

### Example: Connector

In the early stages of setting up our business, we were introduced to Alan, an Irish entrepreneur. Alan had spent several years as CEO of a technology venture. Through that role, and other entrepreneurial ventures in the past, Alan had gradually accrued a huge network in technology, government and the university sector.

At our first meeting with Alan, neither of us had met him before, and he knew little about our business other than that we claimed to be experts on networks. Alan described his network and asked us how he could make it work for him commercially. He knew his network was valuable, but he wanted to know how to monetise it.

But then, almost despite himself, his true Connector instincts came out. It was a Friday afternoon in Dublin, and after our meeting Alan was on his way to the pub for a monthly catch-up with some friends. As we talked, Alan spotted an opportunity to introduce us to Patrick, one of these friends, whom he thought might be a potential client of our work. He asked if we were free, and invited us along to the pub. Over a pint of Guinness, he carefully explained to Patrick how we might be able to help him. At the time, our business was very new and our proposition was raw. Andrew facilitated the conversation between us and Patrick, helping us frame the questions to ask of Patrick, and showing Patrick the value we could offer to him.

Another example of a Connector comes from Mark, Sales director of a UK subsidiary of an Internet advertising company. Mark's team managed the sales relationships in the UK, and the client services and operations were handled in Ireland. Sometimes, advertisements were automatically blocked because they were thought to violate company policy, when this was not in fact the case. Blocked ads caused loss in revenues both for Mark's clients and for his own company. Addressing these violations quickly was vital, and when it happened, Mark needed to reach the right person in Ireland to let them know the problem needed to be solved.

Mark would turn to Kieran, head of the Irish business. Kieran had been in the company a long time and, as a lively and outgoing boss, was well known and liked. According to Mark, Kieran would put in a quick call to ask the right person to listen to what Mark had to say. Without Kieran's intervention, Mark would have to work through the formal channels, and that would take time. By opening a door, Kieran makes it easier for Mark to make the connections he needs.

The interesting aspect of this story is that Mark has not chosen to build the relationships with the approvals team himself. Instead, he relies on the good relationships that Kieran already enjoys. This strategy is effective in a crisis, but is somewhat short-term. Over time, if the problem became endemic, Kieran might start to resent being used in this way. Relationships with Connectors are delicate, as we explore below.

## How to start a conversation with a Connector

As part of my …

[Describe your project or idea or goal.]

It would be very helpful to meet/involve/pitch to … [Name a person or type of person.] … because … [Explain why this introduction would be valuable and what it could lead to.]

Would you be willing to make an introduction for me?  Here is some information about me and my project that you could tell them …

[Provide relevant information, succinctly, perhaps in the form of an email to forward. This makes the Connector's job easier.]

I appreciate that you will want to ask for their agreement first, and will understand if either you or they have reasons not to follow up on this request just at this moment.

## What is implicit in the ask?

When you make a request to a Connector, you are asking to benefit from their reputation. Their introduction is a signal that they think you are worth knowing, and that you have something interesting or useful to offer. In a way, you are 'borrowing' their social capital. It's not just your relationship with the Connector that is at stake, but also their relationship with the person they introduced you to.

For that reason, the 'double opt-in' is becoming more common. Connectors will ask both parties if they are willing to be introduced, before putting them in touch. It is very important that you try to demonstrate that you do, indeed, have something to offer. Follow up on their introduction promptly. Be sure to thank the Connector and let them know the outcome.

Natural Connectors often make unsolicited connections. They spot an opportunity to bring people together and cannot resist doing so. Sometimes these are valuable; other times they may not hit the spot. Either way, do the Connector the courtesy of following up, even if only briefly, and let the Connector know the outcome, and that you are grateful for their intention.

Connectors are very aware of the value their networks represent to others. Several times, we have heard Connectors idly speculate about how they could capture some of the value they create through introductions, as in our example of Alan above. We know one or two Connectors who have figured out ways to do this and are perfectly open about the fact they expect a commission on any business they help to generate. Others are simply happen to make things happen for others. Try to be aware of your Connector's motivation, and act with integrity. Acknowledge the value they bring, and do not be tempted to short-change them.

## Ask yourself:

- How can you make it as easy as possible for your Connector to make a well-informed introduction? What stories do you want them to tell about you?
- Can you send a short paragraph summarising yourself and your opportunity, for the Connector to forward? Is this as relevant as possible?
- Are you at risk of over-reliance on your Connector's reputation? What can you do to build your own?
- What motivates your Connectors to make introductions on your behalf? Are you at risk of using up their goodwill?
- Have you reported back to a Connector on introductions they made on your behalf? What would they enjoy knowing about?

# Summary of Chapter 7

Power roles allow you to get things done, and to reach people and opportunities you would not otherwise be able to access.

**Unlockers** are powerful in providing access to resources that you or your team need to get things done.

**Sponsors** speak out to endorse you to senior people and important gatekeepers.

**Influencers** work behind the scenes to win support and help you get things done. They are able to do this because they are respected by others.

**Connectors** set up introductions in a warm and informative way that makes the new relationship likely to succeed.

# 8 The development roles

*He that wrestles with us strengthens our nerves and sharpens our skill.*

Edmund Burke, Irish statesman and philosopher[37]

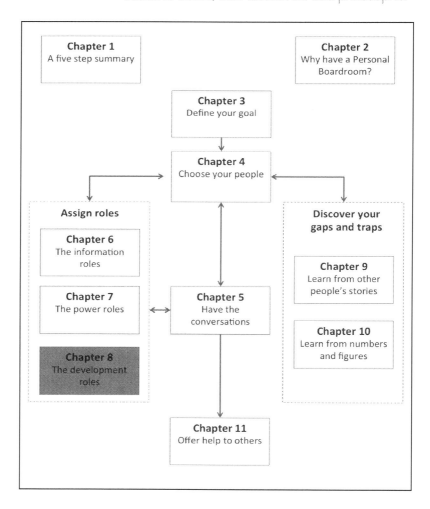

In this chapter we consider the four Development roles in your Personal Boardroom. Development roles give you the self-knowledge to be better at what you do, and to come across at your most powerful to others. Your Improvers give honest appraisals and feedback on your work, and Challengers help you see your blind spots and challenge your arguments to make them better. Your Nerve-Givers and Anchors give you courage, hold you to account for looking after yourself, and remind you to be true to yourself and your values.

As in the previous two chapters, we consider the primary job associated with this role, and what kind of person you might look to. We give examples, offer suggestions about how to start a conversation with the role in mind, and explore what is implicit when you ask someone to take on each role.

## Improver

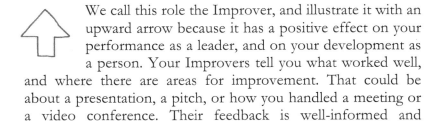 We call this role the Improver, and illustrate it with an upward arrow because it has a positive effect on your performance as a leader, and on your development as a person. Your Improvers tell you what worked well, and where there are areas for improvement. That could be about a presentation, a pitch, or how you handled a meeting or a video conference. Their feedback is well-informed and supported by clear examples and evidence drawn from paying careful attention to what you do.

> *An Improver provides feedback that contributes to your performance as a leader, and your development as a person.*

Your Improvers are people who understand the value of constructive feedback. Most likely, they are self-improvers themselves, so they appreciate the insights and the improvement that can result from being told what could be done better. They are able to provide feedback and to offer development advice in a candid, straightforward way in which emotion is put to one side. They resist snap judgments in favour of suggestions that are supported by evidence.

## Example: Improver

Cathy, a UK-based managing director, told us about Doug, one of her team members who was a very useful Improver. Early in their working relationship, Cathy noticed that Doug was the kind of person who seeks feedback himself, and that he had a knack for observing and articulating what others do well. Cathy asked him to do the same for her after all-hands presentations, and in communicating about the company to the whole business. She asked Doug to give her feedback on what hit the target, and what didn't work so well.

Another Managing Director, Tom, didn't have any Improvers in his Personal Boardroom when he first used our diagnostic tool. We explored with him whether there was anyone in his team who could provide more direct and immediate feedback on how he comes across. He identified Kate, the business manager for his team, as someone who knows what is going on and how things are received. He had a sufficient level of trust to feel comfortable about inviting her feedback, without feeling he was putting her in a difficult position.

## How to start a conversation with an Improver

I'm doing a ... [Insert presentation/speech/communication/meeting—and say when it is happening]

I'd like to know how it is received, and how well I handle it. It is sometimes hard for me to perceive that for myself. Would you be willing to take notes for me, and sit down with me afterwards and talk me through them? I would really appreciate it if you could note down some examples, as well as giving your general impression.

OR

> In the next quarter, I'm going to focus on improving my …
>
> [Mention what it is you are focusing on.]
>
> I know there are some things I could be better at. Could you help me understand some of those things a little better?

## What is implicit in the ask?

You are asking your Improver to be honest and to tell you about your mistakes and mishandling of situations, as well as the things that go well. Prepare for the fact that they may touch on areas that you feel vulnerable about. If they are worried about hurting your feelings, their role as an Improver will not be effective, so you need to keep emotion out of the conversation. Keep the conversation focused on specific examples, which are easier to talk about objectively than broad-brush impressions. Do not ask someone who is likely to trigger an emotional response in you.

Try to be very clear about the boundaries of when you are open to feedback, and what about. That might sound like you are limiting the conversation, but actually it is important, especially if your Improver is junior to you. Give them some warning about upcoming events or communications that you want feedback on, and schedule a time to meet to talk about it. It helps to signal when you are ready to receive feedback or suggestions, and when you want others to provide it, so that they don't feel they are expected to do it all the time.

Make direct requests for it, rather than assuming people will provide it. The least effective way is to say just once 'I like feedback,' and then never ask again. More effective is to invite it once and then encourage people to keep it coming. Most effective of all is to signal that you want it on specific occasions, so that your Improver can do his or her job well.

Avoid the temptation to rebuff feedback or make excuses for observed weaknesses, and always thank your Improver for his/her viewpoint, even if you disagree.

### Ask yourself:

- Is your boss included in your list of Improvers. Especially when you are new to role, asking your boss how to improve can make the difference to whether or not you are successful.
- Is there a direct report in your list of Improvers? Would it help to have their immediate feedback? How can you make it safe for them to be honest with you?
- How can you create the conditions in which feedback can be given honestly, drawing on clear examples, without putting the Improver in a difficult position, or triggering an emotional response in you?
- If your team is in different locations, is there an Improver in each location?

## Challenger

 We call this role the Challenger, and illustrate it with a hazard sign, because this role calls attention to your blind spots and breaks you out of habitual ways of seeing the world.

While the Improver is concerned with your effectiveness as a person, the Challenger is someone who engages with your ideas. This is not always an agreeable role or a supportive one. In fact your Challengers can be quite difficult individuals, or people who make your life uncomfortable. But there is usually a good outcome: as a consequence of talking to a Challenger, you are able to produce a clearer argument, a better pitch or presentation, a more convincing piece of writing or a more compelling story; or to drop a bad idea before taking it too far.

*Challengers make your thinking more productive, and your arguments more persuasive and compelling.*

Your Challengers are valuable to you because they process information in a different way, or see the world through an unusual lens, or represent a different set of values from your own. In explaining or defending your own position, you learn how other people evaluate and interpret what you say. Whether or not you agree, Challengers open your mind to other points of view. Used well, they make your thinking more productive, and your arguments more persuasive and compelling.

## Example: Challenger

Monica, a litigation lawyer, named a client as her Challenger. George, an in-house lawyer in a large petrochemicals organisation, made her life difficult. George was quick to point out flaws in her reasoning and disagree with advice. Although Monica's position was to act as his professional advisor— brought in to look after the interests of his company—she often felt she was fighting against him more than supporting him. She had to prepare for every meeting with immense care, making sure she had an argument to support every piece of advice she offered. That meant poring over prior legal precedents and cases with even greater breadth and depth than usual.

Over time, Monica learned to anticipate what he was likely to object to, and how to head off his concerns before he expressed them. Her comment was that, because he placed such demands on her, she became a better litigator as a result. And later, when she was applying for partnership in her firm, she said that George was one of the clients who most supportive of her business case.

People sometimes become known for representing a particular customer group or user perspective. One entrepreneur we know has a non-executive director who expects to see user data to support every business decision. Knowing this, our friend has taken to anticipating these data requests. In doing so, he has found that he has started to make better decisions himself, coming to appreciate the perspective user data can bring.

## How to start a conversation with a Challenger

With my team, I'm working on a project or idea that will ...

[Explain the broad objective that you are aiming for, or your vision, to help your Challenger see the bigger picture.]

Our success depends on being really good at ...

[Explain the specific domain of expertise you need help with.]

We have been working on this for a while, and have created some great material, but I'm aware that we could really benefit from getting a fresh perspective on this, from someone who doesn't necessarily think like we do, or represents a different point of view.

As someone who is ...

[Mention the expertise or knowledge that the Challenger has.]

... would you mind giving me some detailed comments on how this come across to you, and all the ways it could be improved?

[Explain exactly what you are asking them to do, and by when.]

## What is implicit in the ask?

You are asking your Challenger to give you their response to an issue or decision or a case you are dealing with. They will scrutinise your approach, test your judgment and appraise the robustness of your argument. To set this up well, explain what it is about their experience or mindset that is valuable to you. Is it knowledge of a market, or their instinct for how customers think? Are you looking for detailed feedback on a slide deck, or better ways of wording emails?

A good Challenger is someone with very high standards for their own work. They expect others to have high standards too. They want to know that you have done everything in your power to make the work as good as it can be before getting them involved. If you work is in draft form or half-finished, be sure to signal this, because they will not look kindly on you if they think this is the finished article.

Also, be very clear about what you are asking them to do, and by when. Do you want comments, detailed edits, suggestions, new ideas or overall impressions? What form do you want to receive this in?

## Ask yourself:

- Where are your Challengers drawn from? Is there someone outside your team who can help you avoid the groupthink that results from working closely together?
- How can you maximise the value your Challengers offer, by being very clear about what you want from them? Can you make it easier for them to do their job by giving them more background information and sharing the bigger picture?
- What specialist knowledge do your Challengers have? How can you play to their strengths?

# Nerve-Giver

 We call this role the Nerve-Giver, and illustrate it with a syringe because this role builds self-belief when you have taken a knock, and gives you resolve when you are feeling nervous about a bold action. They build confidence, and help you hang on to a sense of purpose at times when you feel anxious or defeated.

*Nerve-Givers give you confidence to continue when things are difficult, and to build resolve to take a bold action.*

They do this in various ways: by talking through something in a rational way when you are feeling emotional; by reminding you of things you have said in the past; or simply by being beside you and believing in you.

Nerve-Givers can come from any part of your life—your team, part of your company, former colleagues, your parents, children, siblings or spouse, a user or beneficiary of your product or service, *etc.* They are often the first people you turn to when you have a major set-back. They know you and your situation well enough to make shrewd observations, remind you about choices you made, and call you out when you are being unfair on yourself.

## Example: Nerve-Giver

James, a helicopter pilot in the military, gave an example of a boss who was a Nerve-Giver. His unit was asked to participate in a mission in Afghanistan which involved flying his light helicopter close to an enemy position in broad daylight to cover it, while a larger helicopter disembarked ground troops. James felt that this mission would expose him and his crew to an unnecessary risk, and that two covering helicopters would be safer. To propose this to a senior office would be to go against protocol, and could be seen as insubordination. He also worried that his senior officer would view him as risk-averse, which would reflect badly on his service as an officer.

James sought the advice of a former boss, Michael, who had developed attack strategies for many years. Michael asked him whether the senior officer had a sufficient appreciation of the risk. The senior officer did not understand the risks as fully as James and his team. Michael asked whether the senior officer was aware of the signals he was giving to those undertaking the mission about how their welfare was viewed. Michael suggested that, although the operation *could* be undertaken with only one cover helicopter, James might consider whether it *should* be done in that way.

This conversation with Michael gave James the courage to challenge the senior officer about his appraisal of the risks. He tactfully suggested that the welfare of the crew was a matter of principle, and the increased presence from two helicopters would make the enemy think twice about engaging them. The senior office changed his mind, even though the operation had to be delayed slightly in order to procure a second aircraft. The aim was achieved without incident. Michael's advice has become a model for James' resolve in situations where it takes moral courage to do things the right way.

In his book, Ben Horowitz described how board member Bill Campbell acted as a Nerve-Giver on a number of occasions. One was towards the end of 2000, when Loudcloud was running out of money, and the private funding market had practically shut down on making new investments. Nonetheless, Ben had the bold idea of seeking an IPO. He presented the options to the board, boldly stating all the reasons why going public would be very difficult. The board listened quietly. Horowitz described what happened when Bill Campbell broke the silence:

"'Ben, it's not the money."

'I felt a strange sense of relief. Maybe we didn't have to go public. ... Perhaps there was another way.

'Then Bill spoke again, "It's the *fucking* money."

'"Okay, I guess we are going public."'[38]

## How to start a conversation with a Nerve-Giver

> I wondered if you could spare some time to talk something through with me.
>
> I'm in a difficult situation because ...
>
> [Give some background.]
>
> As a consequence I/we have taken the decision to / need to take a decision about ...
>
> [Explain what actions you have taken or need to take.]
>
> I want to be sure I/we are doing the right thing. Would you mind helping me think this through?

## What is implicit in the ask?

This is not a role that involves giving advice. A good Nerve-Giver is not someone who tells you what he or she would do in your situation, or turns the conversation around to talking about themselves. A Nerve-giver reflects back to you what they hear you saying, and helps you clarify the reasons for the path you have taken, or want to take. They remind you why a decision is necessary, or prompt you to live up to standards you set for yourself.

Sometimes, they are willing to put into words a bald truth that you are reluctant to say or hear, like Bill Campbell did for Ben Horowitz. Sometimes it is their strong adherence to a certain way of working that provides a reference point for you, as in the case of James and his former boss. By doing more listening than talking, they give you the opportunity to hear your own voice, and work yourself through to the right solution.

## Ask yourself:

- Have you chosen Nerve-Givers who are good listeners? Will they listen first, before jumping in to tell you what to do, or proposing solutions before you have had time to work things through?
- Do your Nerve-Givers understand your values and what you stand for? What stories can you share about yourself to help them know you better?

## Anchor

 We call this role the Anchor, because this role keeps you connected to the bedrock on which your life is built. You may have to voyage on stormy seas and navigate unknown waters, but at anchor you are able to relax and recharge. At the same time an anchor keeps you from straying when you are off-guard. Anchors remind you when you are not looking after yourself or people important to you. They care about your physical, mental, spiritual and emotional health.

*An Anchor is someone concerned for your wellbeing. Look for Anchors in your workplace as well as at home.*

This is a role that people often step into because they care about you. That is especially the case for spouses, partners, other family members and friends, who have a deep concern for your wellbeing, and want to be sure work doesn't impinge unduly on that.

However, we think you should also be looking for Anchors at work too, especially if you are in a very demanding job. You might ask a colleague to insist that you leave work when it really matters, or to create space in your diary for that to happen. That could be your assistant, your boss, or someone at the next desk.

## Example: Anchor

Ben Horowitz recounted a joke his father made, which was not really a joke. This was early in Ben's career, when he did not earn much, and his family were sweltering in a house without air-conditioning. This is how he described their conversation:

'My father turned to me and said "Son, do you know what's cheap?"

'Since I had absolutely no idea what he was talking about, I replied "No, what?"

'"Flowers. Flowers are really cheap. But do you know what's expensive?" he asked.

'Again, I replied "No, what?"

'He said 'Divorce.'" [39]

At that point, Ben had realised that, if he continued on the course he was on, he might lose his family.

We have heard many other lovely stories about Anchors: a male executive who meets up with three school friends and they tease each other mercilessly; a female executive who has a long-standing arrangement with a group of friends to meet for a weekend every three months: *No partners, no children, just us. I love it.*

## How to start a conversation with an Anchor

> The next few weeks/months are going to be a very demanding period at work ... [Explain why.]
>
> As you know, having time for ... [my children / spouse / exercise / hobbies / church] ... is very important to me. I desperately want to be able to do some of that, even though I'll be in the office most of the time.
>
> As a colleague who I trust and respect, would you be willing to help me ring-fence some time or space for this by ...
>
> [Explain what actions you want the person to take.]
>
> And will you remind me by asking me once a day/week how I'm doing? If I know you're checking up on me/looking out for me, that will stop me losing track of time/allowing my diary to fill up/forgetting what's important.

## What is implicit in the ask?

You are asking your Anchor to let you know when they think you're not looking after yourself or being true to what is important to you. Your colleagues may not feel this is any of their business, especially where it concerns your family or your health. But to achieve the balance you seek, it can be very helpful if people at work understand your priorities. People at home are naturally vocal about the work-life balance of their partners or parents. To find such people at work, you might need to invite them to take this job on.

Anchors must be people who are not overwhelmed by your success, and who are able to be honest and to point out home truths. That might be because they see you gaining or losing weight, or because you haven't been around much, or because you are not smiling as much as you used to. Your Anchor makes it clear, quietly or loudly depending on their personality, that they are looking out for you.

There are times when an Anchor's reminders are not welcome, or are difficult to hear. Life circumstances do change, and sometimes values change too. You might feel you have moved on; but the most caring friends stay with you even as you change—so cherish them and listen when it counts.

## Ask yourself:

- Do I have an Anchor outside work who can understand the pressures I'm under at work?
- Do I have an Anchor inside work, who will help me keep parts of my day free?
- Is someone reminding me that this job is not for ever, and that one day I won't be needed here any more?
- Am I reluctant to listen to my Anchor? Is that because they are telling me something I don't want to hear?

# Summary of Chapter 8

Development roles give you the self-knowledge to be better at what you do, and to come across at your most powerful to others.

**Improvers** give candid, constructive feedback on your performance and development.

**Challengers** make your thinking more productive, and your arguments more persuasive and compelling.

**Nerve-Givers** strengthen your resolve at difficult times, and give you a sense of purpose.

**Anchors** are concerned for your well-being. Look for Anchors in your workplace as well as at home.

# 9 Learn from other people's stories

*We learn best—and change—from hearing stories that strike a chord within us.*

John Kotter [40]

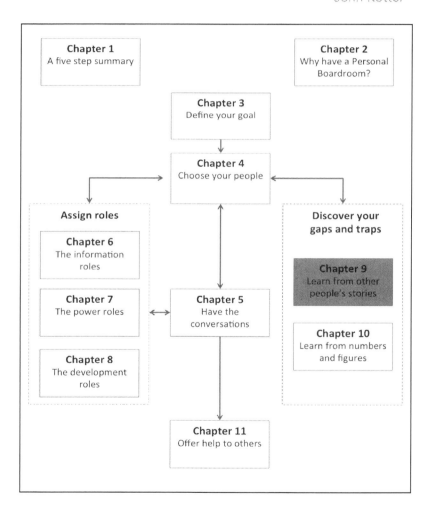

We have worked with hundreds of executives on their Personal Boardrooms. In this chapter, we tell some stories of people we have worked with whose Boardrooms illustrate common traps and gaps, and explain some of the ways we have been able to help them identify and cultivate opportunities. All names and distinguishing details have been changed.

If one of these stories strikes a chord, we hope it will provide a way for you to reflect on whether or not you have the right Personal Boardroom.


## The bingo boss

Sally has worked in retail for three decades. She began in a local store in her home town in the southern US, after she left high school, and then worked her way up through the learning and development function, first as a trainer herself, and later managing a group of trainers. Sally's team were responsible for designing in-house training for front-line staff, and for delivering training in stores throughout the US.

During her career, Sally twice experienced her company being acquired as a result of industry consolidation. The first time, after the initial upheaval, there was little change to how training was run. We met Sally just after the second merger. This time, the acquiring company had a very different learning and development strategy from Sally's company.

We worked with Sally as she made the transition into a new role. She was to be responsible for making training available to the front-line operation, but not for design or delivery of it. All front-line training was outsourced to a third-party supplier.

When we work with people in transition, we find it helpful to introduce people to a structured way of thinking about networks by first applying that thinking to a role they are deeply familiar with. We did this with Sally by mapping her Personal Boardroom in her old role before her company was acquired.

It became quickly apparent that Sally's former boss, Lorraine, ticked all the boxes. She was deeply knowledgeable in learning and development, and very well connected in the business. She knew who did what, and how to get things done. She was good at channelling people to Sally's team and then stepping back to giving Sally plenty of space to deliver.

Lorraine was a bingo boss. The bingo boss is someone who plays most or all of the twelve roles. He or she is a fount of information, unlocks resources, opens doors, looks out for you, speaks out on your behalf, offers useful feedback, challenges your thinking and reminds you to take care of your work-life balance.

*'Lorraine was the one resource I would always go to' – Sally.*

As a consequence of the merger, Lorraine did not stay with the company. She and Sally remained close, and they still met regularly for dinner, but Sally had lost a trusted boss who had created a environment in which she could excel. Re-establishing that level of support in the new organisation was hard, especially as Sally's physical location was distant from her new boss Lorenzo and his team. Six months into the new role, Sally was still working out how to surmount the us-and-them feeling that often accompanies a merger, and to earn Lorenzo's trust and respect.

## What to do if you have a bingo boss

If you have such a boss, he or she is a gift to treasure while you can. But when you or your boss moves on, there is a risk that your Personal Boardroom will feel very empty.

First, make the most of the bingo boss. She is playing many different roles in your Personal Boardroom. Find ways to structure conversations so that you really can draw down all the benefits she can offer. Schedule time for a conversation about how to navigate the organisation, and who your boss could connect you to (acting as Navigator and Connector). Ask for feedback regularly (Improver) and in every one-on-one meeting ask her to comment on something you are working on to make it more effective (Challenger). Make her aware of your career goals (Sponsor) but do this at some other time than when you are talking about resource needs (Unlocker) or how she can help you get things done (Influencer).

Second, do some succession planning. A superstar boss may well move on to another role. For each role that she plays, find one other person to play that role too. Balance her perspective with someone else's. You might find that other people see and do things rather differently. Having new perspectives from others will not only reduce your dependence on your boss, but may also mean you have more to offer her in return.

## The empty Boardroom

Jane works for a venture that runs career-development programmes for leaders and managers in social enterprises. She agreed to complete our diagnostic as she thought it might be a useful addition to her programme. Completing the assessment probably felt like a formality.

But when she looked at her results, Jane got a surprise. She saw a large number of undifferentiated names (because she had entered groups of people rather than individuals). There were few people playing clear roles, and she had no Inspirers, Unlockers, Connectors or Nerve-Givers. The majority of her relationships were categorised as distant or shallow, which meant that her Personal Boardroom was sorely lacking the supportive value deep and strong ties can bring.

In a coaching session, Jane tried to answer some probing questions about who she had selected and where they fitted. After a pause, she said *I don't think this is a question of making alterations to what's there. This is fundamental. I don't have a Personal Boardroom to start with. I look at this and I feel that I have been very naïve. I've never reached out to people to help me. It's always been about my work, which is about other people and their needs.*

As the implications of the results began to sink in, Jane became frustrated and cross. She expressed envy of others who had built their careers in a deliberate way. Because she had not been deliberate, people in her professional world hadn't delivered opportunities for her that she thought she would be given. Jane said: *I advocate network building for others but you know, I don't practice what I preach.*

> '*I don't have a Personal Boardroom to start with. I feel that I have been very naïve. I've never reached out to people to help me.*' – Jane

Fired up, Jane wanted to take action. She identified a career goal—a promotion she sought in the next six months—and prioritised the roles she felt would be most important to focus on. These included:

- **A Sponsor**. This would be her boss, but she recognised the conversation needed to change. She resolved to be explicit about her intentions.
- **An Influencer**. This would be a new director on the board she needed to get closer to and ask for support.
- **A Nerve-Giver**. Regular lunches with her friend 'Just-do-it George' would be needed.
- **An Inspirer** to energise her and fill her up with possibilities and ideas.

### What to do if you have an empty Boardroom

Perhaps, like Jane, you have never been comfortable about asking other people for help. Maybe you've never tried building your career in a deliberate way. If that is the case, then perhaps you picked up this book without the first idea of who to include in your Personal Boardroom.

Start with a review of the relationships you currently rely on (your boss, team members, senior managers, a mentor) and think about whether these people play any roles for you. If these relationships are shallow (frequent, but low in trust and not close), consider how to invest in the relationship to build trust. That might mean being willing to be more open about your own needs, or it might be simply spending more time learning about people—what they like and enjoy doing, their background, what makes them laugh, *etc.*

Where you have role gaps, use the tools in Chapter 4 to think divergently about who might fill them. Then use the conversation-starters in Chapters 6 to 8 to initiate contact. As you start having the conversations, your sense of having people to support you will grow. And if you are someone who, like Jane, has always looked at other people's needs rather than your own, follow some of the suggestions in Chapter 11: carry on being a giver, but do so in a way that builds your reputation.

## The inside Boardroom

Anil is the marketing director of a global technology company, on a mission to deliver transformational change for its customers. It's fast-paced, complex and totally engrossing. He can eat, rest and exercise all within a few metres of his desk, and external visitors will come out of their way to see his offices, so he barely has a need to leave the building.

When Anil completed a Personal Boardroom diagnostic, he filled it with a variety of specialists, from different functional areas and in a variety of locations around the world. The diagnostic made him aware just how many people he could reach from his desk.

It also made him realise that what he lacked was the breadth and freshness of perspective that people *outside* the organisation could bring—all but one of his relationships were internal.

Anil quickly saw the trap he'd fallen into, and he wanted to rethink where he was investing his time. He wasn't short of people he could reach out to; he was friendly and easy-going, and naturally drew people to himself. But his company was so high-profile that he was accustomed to being the one others wanted to probe for insights. He recognised that he needed to reverse the direction of these conversations so that he could put himself in outsiders' shoes and ask the questions. He identified three people to act as Inspirer, Navigator and Expert, who could help him spot new ideas and create winning partnerships for his customers.

## What to do if you have an inside Boardroom

Consider the value that an external perspective can bring. How do you customers think? Who in another company or industry has done something similar to a challenge you now face—whether that's a people challenge, a search technology solution, or a supply chain problem? What could you learn from talking to someone doing something vastly different, but inspiring?

For Anil, the biggest obstacle to making this happen was getting out of the building. How much easier it was to eat the free food on hand than to have to find the exit first. But Anil recognised that getting out of the building was vital for seeing his company through the eyes of others. He resolved to do this from now on at least one day a week.

Consider what you might gain by doing the same. Could you earmark a certain point in the week—a lunchtime or breakfast—for meeting someone outside? And, for people further afield, would technology help? Could you find low-friction ways of connecting with people who are distant, through Skype or Hangouts?

## The outsider

Nicola worked in new business sales for a technology company known for hiring highly analytical people. Most of her seniors were former management consultants. Nicola, on the other hand, described herself as coming from a 'hunting background' in sales. She perceived this distinction very acutely, feeling that her face did not fit. Her previous boss had told Nicola that she would never be considered for promotion. Her current boss was impressed by Nicola hitting her revenue goals, but Nicola was still not sure he would consider her for the next level up.

When Nicola saw her Personal Boardroom diagnostic report, in which we use colour to differentiate people according to their career background, it was very apparent that every member was very different from her. Everyone in her Personal Boardroom, apart from her spouse and a sibling, was a senior colleague with a consulting background. There were people more like Nicola in other parts of the sales organisation, but she did not consider them for her Boardroom.

> *'We are very focused on our specific markets in my company, so why would other sales people want to talk to me?' – Nicola*

She did not include any of her direct reports either. Nicola commented that they were also from a 'hunting background', and that as she was ambitious to succeed in a world of management consultants, she didn't think her team could help her with that challenge.

Nicola perceived herself as a outsider trying to succeed in a world where her face didn't fit. She described her challenge to us as this: how to wield influence in a world where senior people have a very different career background from herself.

As we talked through the promotion she wanted, she understood the value of including people similar to herself in her Personal Boardroom. They may have found ways of dealing with being outsiders, or they may not perceive a different background to be a problem. Either way, she could learn from them. She also resolved to use the promotion as a pretext to have more purposeful conversations with people who could be Sponsors and Influencers.

## What to do if you are an outsider

From Chapter 4 you will know that we encouraged you to think about the diversity of your Personal Boardroom; and one of the measures we suggested you think about was their career background. We asked you to rate how similar or different each person is—relative to you—in terms of their education, and the industries and jobs they have been involved with in the past. You may be aware that your Personal Boardroom is full of people who are very different from you.

First, consider whether you might include some colleagues who are similar to you—other people in a similar job, or people who have made a transition like yours. They might have experienced some of the issues you are now facing, giving them a useful insight which you could learn from (as an Expert or Improver). They may have felt like outsiders themselves, and worked out how to deal with that. Or they might have developed strategies for communicating with people in a certain job or function or level of seniority. (If so, they might be a helpful Challenger or

Nerve-Giver.) Try to build connections with some people who are similar to you.

*Connect on similarity, benefit from difference.*[41]

It is often easier to establish a high-quality relationship if you have some common ground to begin with. From there, you can branch out to make sense of the situation you're in, while still holding on to the frame of reference and vocabulary you share because of your background. Consider whether people outside your business, or in a different part of the organisation, who have a similar training or background to yours, could be useful Boardroom members.

## The stale Boardroom

We met Rachel, a programme manager for an Internet company. Prior to a maternity leave, she ran a sales team. After she returned, her job changed. She become part of a three-year project on customer segmentation and service design. The business had also changed. Two of the leaders who previously looked out for her moved on. People who were previously peers were now more senior. The majority of her present work was with a virtual team, and her boss was based in another country. When she was in a sales role, she had been visible to senior managers all the time. Now, her only visibility was when she took a proposal to a senior manager for approval.

Looking at her Personal Boardroom diagnostic report, Rachel knew her Boardroom needed to change. She needed to rekindle contact with former bosses who were in her local office: people she used to know well who would be Influencers for her new project. She needed to find opportunities to connect more frequently with the senior managers who were Influencers or Unlockers. She recognised that her peers were missing. She decided to connect with others in programme management roles who could be Experts and Navigators for her as she learned the role.

## What to do if you have a stale Boardroom

One of the wake-up calls a Personal Boardroom diagnostic tool gives people like Rachel is the realisation that their Boardroom is out of date. All careers go through phases, and it is appropriate to refresh your Personal Boardroom from time to time. Letting go of some people who no longer fill a role for you will create space for conversations that are more appropriate to your current situation.

You might find it helpful to do some experimental thinking. Come up with a specific, targeted goal for your Personal Boardroom (see Chapter 3) and plan who to include in your Boardroom to help you achieve that. Or think about who, if you were being your most ambitious, would be the ideal group of people to help you be a truly effective leader (see Chapter 4 on ways to come up with a long-list). Add some of these names to an 'outer circle' list if you don't feel your relationship with them is ready for inclusion in your Personal Boardroom. Then look for opportunities to get to know them and let them know more about what you do.

# The outpost

When Sarah, a VP of Learning and Development in a global travel business headquartered in the US, gave us her Personal Boardroom data we were surprised to see that every single member of her Boardroom worked in a different country. Sarah is based in Ireland, and the people who report to her are scattered around the world. Her boss is based in Geneva and is constantly travelling. The company is headquartered in the US. So it is perhaps not surprising that all of her Personal Boardroom members were overseas.

However, being an outpost does present challenges. Most day-to-day business in Sarah's company is conducted *via* phone or video conference; but you have to work hard to stay front-of-mind. Sarah said about her boss 'The thing about virtual working is, you have less visibility and they don't see you operate around other people. So it's harder to get feedback. And you have to battle for share of mind.' Sarah uses instant messaging as the virtual equivalent of putting her head around someone's office door, firing off the occasional casual message when she sees someone is online. She has become accustomed to this way of working.

> *'After 15 years in the company, I know more people in my profession in the US than in Ireland, where I live.' – Sarah*

Her bigger challenge is how to build a Personal Boardroom for her next role. She is looking for an opportunity in her home country—but her network is heavily US-centric. We helped Sarah think about adding Navigators and Connectors based in Ireland and the UK—people who could help her build her network for the next stage of her career.

## What to do if you are an outpost

If, like Sarah, most of your Personal Boardroom members are overseas, you will know how hard it is to make sure you're visible to people who matter, to get feedback, and to stay at the front of people's minds. Make sure you keep up with Navigators who can keep you up to date with trends in policy or priorities, and work hard to cultivate relationships with Sponsors and Influencers in locations where key decisions are made.

Because opportunities for face-to-face interaction are limited, your digital communications are all the more important. Building and sustaining trust is that much harder when relationships are over a distance, so making sure that digital communications convey the right tone and intent is important.

We like to talk about digital body language—how you come across on email. Simple things like spelling, capitalisation, abbreviations, line breaks, paragraph breaks, and opening and closing statements make a difference to how your message is received. Think about the emails you get: which ones are effective? What can you learn from the people who are really good at digital communication? Could one of these people be an Expert for you?

## The inherited Boardroom

We worked with Neil in his first 90 days of an international transition. Formerly CFO of the Canadian subsidary of a global company, he moved to London to head the finance division in the UK, reporting to the Global CFO.

Finance was seen in a negative way in the UK business, and Neil wanted to change that, as he had done in Canada. The obvious starting point for his new Personal Boardroom was the relationships he had inherited in the new role: his boss, his team and his peers. Amongst his peers he found himself caught between two cliques, invited to dinners where each group talked about the other.

His new boss Mark, UK CEO, was critical to his success, but Neil needed to work out how to manage him. Meetings with Mark went on for an hour or two longer than scheduled, much to Neil's frustration. Andrew, a direct report, was someone who knew the UK business inside-out and was very well connected. But there was tension between them, as Andrew considered himself as a candidate for Neil's role. Neil recognised that he needed to develop Andrew as his successor (to be an Improver and Challenger for him) but in the first instance, he said 'I need to further leverage him to gain detailed knowledge.'

In his first few months, there were few relationships that were where he wanted them to be, and many shallow ties that needed to become deeper. One of these was Juan, at least until the evening when Juan came to drinks and stayed until late. After their heart-to-heart, Neil felt he could be straight with Juan:

*'Now that I've been out until 3 am with Juan, it's easier to tell him what I need: bullet points, not 40 pages of data!'* – *Neil*

One of the most difficult inherited relationships was with his PA, Charlotte. He was frustrated by the way his previous boss tolerated an outmoded way of working—with Charlotte just printing mounds of paper, making cups of tea and getting him lunch. 'I need someone who can anticipate what's happening, be flexible and change on the fly, and manage the people who are filing my diary. Charlotte is not an Influencer; she keeps herself to herself.'

## What to do if you have an inherited Boardroom

In the early days of a new role, you might feel that trust and openness are fairly low. It's likely that your Personal Boardroom members will be shallow ties to start with: people you see frequently but do not feel close to. (See Chapter 4 for more on shallow ties.)

Neil found our sessions helpful for taking stock of these inherited relationships, and for figuring out who he could trust, and for what. You can do the same by periodically taking time out to think about the people around you. Neil was aware that there were many people he needed to get closer to. Keep a list of people in your 'outer circle'. Think of this as a waiting area for people outside your Personal Boardroom, who you would like to bring in.

Prompted by our conversations, Neil sat down with his PA and asked her to take a more proactive approach. He was happy to get his own lunch, and if necessary someone else could make tea for visitors. He wanted his PA to manage diary requests so that he had more time with the right people, including meetings with people in his new Personal Boardroom. Consider whether your assistant could do something similar to help you build your network in the first months of a role, and to prioritise time according to a structured approach.

# Summary of Chapter 9

Some of the common patterns we've observed in Personal Boardrooms are:

The **bingo boss**, who plays most or all of the twelve roles. Structure the conversations to make the most of your boss. Do some succession planning.

The **empty Boardroom**, when you have never reached out to people to help you. Start asking, using the 12 roles as an aid to conversation.

The **inside Boardroom**, when the stimulation from inside relationships is so great that you overlook the value of outside perspectives. Make time for external meetings.

The **outsider**, who perceives herself to be different from everyone else. Connect on similarity; benefit from difference.

The **stale Boardroom** is out of date. Release old relationships to make room for new conversations.

The **outpost** is geographically remote from their Personal Boardroom members. Work hard to stay in touch, and be careful with your digital body language.

The **inherited Boardroom** is the one you take on in a new role. Invest in making these shallow ties deeper, and use your PA to help you.

# 10 Learn from numbers and figures

*The greatest value of a picture is when it forces us to notice what we never expected to see.*

John Tukey, American Mathematician [42]

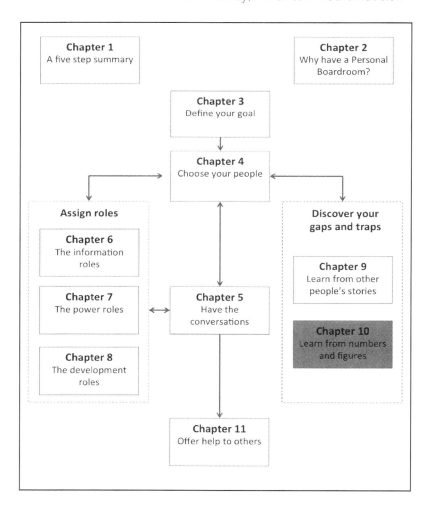

In this chapter we take an analytical view of the whole Personal Boardroom and consider its overall composition. Where are people drawn from? Do you have the right mix of people?

We find that representing data visually often reveals patterns or tendencies that people were previously unaware of. Likewise, applying a score to Personal Boardroom data helps people spot biases and gaps. Our diagnostic tool presents data both visually and in numbers, and here we share some of the techniques we use.

Before this, though, we review some general principles that apply to the composition of your Boardroom.

## The principles of Personal Boardroom composition

### Diversity is good

A diverse Personal Boardroom includes some people who are not too similar to you or to each other. They are drawn from different teams and business units inside your organisation, and from other locations. They are not all sitting on the same floor in the same office as you, but equally they are not all in another country.

*A Personal Boardroom that is diverse is more likely to deliver creative insights, and to link you to a wider-reaching set of connections that extend your capability.*

This does not mean that your Personal Boardroom must be diverse in terms of demographic factors like ethnicity, nationality, age and gender. However, it is important to think carefully about these categories too. If everyone is in your age range, or older, you are missing out on the perspectives of younger people, who may bring a very different approach and mindset to what your business does, or how your employees or customers think. Similarly, if everyone in your Personal Boardroom is the same gender as you, what are you missing?

The Lean In groups advocated by Sheryl Sandberg are a great way for women to support each other.[43] However, if your Lean In group is only composed of other women, and you work in a company where the senior management is predominantly male, you need men in your Personal Boardroom who can represent the expectations of senior management. Likewise, if you are in the majority gender or ethnic group in your business, you might benefit from hearing the perspective of someone from a minority group.

A diverse Personal Boardroom might include a couple of people you do not know well or feel close to. In Chapter 4 we referred to these as shallow ties (people you see regularly but don't feel close to) and distant ties (for people you don't see regularly). Distant ties can be very valuable precisely because they are not wrapped up in the work and issues you deal with every day.

## Balance is good

A balanced Personal Boardroom has each of the information, power and development roles represented in equal proportions. That means you are not under- or over-investing in one of these three areas. We have observed a tendency amongst some people who have completed our Personal Boardroom diagnostic to have a predominance of either development or information roles. They tend to have a low proportion of people in power roles. That suggests they are investing too heavily on self-improvement or on gaining insight, at the expense of getting connected into powerful coalitions and building consensus.

*A balanced Personal Boardroom has each of the information, power and development roles represented in equal proportions.*

A balanced Personal Boardroom also provides more than one viewpoint on an issue. One of the great utilities of a Personal Boardroom is to give you access to people who see things differently from you. That means you might expect to encounter conflicting opinions from time to time. You might receive a piece of information or advice from one person that conflicts with what someone else said. See yourself as the chairperson of this Boardroom, listening to all the voices around the table, and doing so without judgment.

Once you have heard from enough people, then converge on the decision that is right for you. If people have conflicting expectations of you, you will need to manage the expectations of those who see things a different way from you. To achieve that, other Personal Boardroom members may need to act as Sponsors or Influencers to support your decision.

## Visualise your Personal Boardroom

Our Personal Boardroom report is a diagnostic tool that helps people think about whether they have the correct composition and balance in their Boardroom. We use mapping tools to show the composition visually, and use various metrics to summarise the data. We find this works well for people who like the idea of having a score to measure their progress. These visualisations and metrics can help you reflect on the composition and balance of your Personal Boardroom.

In order to generate a Personal Boardroom report, we collect the following information:

- The names of the people in your Personal Boardroom (up to 12 names)
- The role/s each person plays. Each role can have many people assigned to it, and each person can play many roles.
- How close and trusting your relationship is with each person, and how frequently you meet
- Where each person is drawn from (your team, outside your team, outside your business unit or function, outside the company, outside the industry, *etc.*)
- How similar or different each person is to you in the jobs they have had in the past, their professional training, and the industries they have worked in
- Whether each person is senior or junior to you (or one of your peers, if this is applicable)

We use the data to create a report tailored to you, showing both visualisations and metrics. Visual representations can be very powerful for identifying over-reliance on certain types of people, and gaps where people who should be represented are missing. We build up this visual representation up in layers, as shown in the following figures.

Figure 4: Fred's Personal Boardroom map, showing seniority

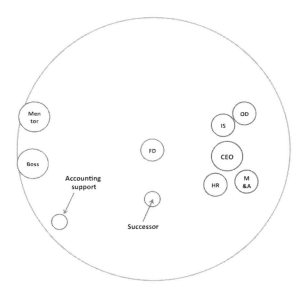

As an example, consider the illustration of a Finance Director's Personal Boardroom shown in Figure 4. It shows the Finance Director in the centre, in a circle with a white background, labelled FD. We'll call him Fred. Around Fred's circle the members of his Boardroom are shown. The size of the circles represents their seniority relative to Fred. More senior people, shown as large circles, include his boss, the CEO of the UK business, and a mentor. People at the same level have a similar-sized circle to Fred. These include the heads of Human Resources (HR) and Organization Development (OD), the head of Mergers and Acquisitions (M&A) and the head of Information Systems (IS). There are two junior people: a direct report who is labelled 'Successor' and someone in Accounting Support.

Figure 5: Fred's Personal Boardroom map, showing career background

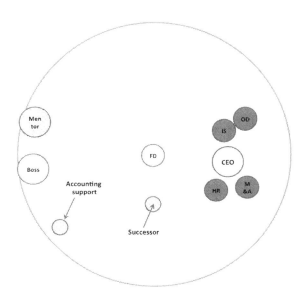

In Figure 5 we add shading to denote career background. The white circles are people with a background very similar to Fred's. These are his boss, who is the European head of finance, and the CEO, who trained with one of the global accounting firms, and worked his way up through various finance and accounting roles. The light grey circles include the mentor, who began his career in finance but moved out into strategy; Fred's successor, a finance guy who did a spell in an operations; and the accounting support person whose background spans finance and systems. The dark-coloured circles are people who have very different career backgrounds.

*Visual representations of a Personal Boardroom, and scores, can be very powerful for identifying diversity and balance.*

Figure 6: Fred's Personal Boardroom map, showing geographic proximity

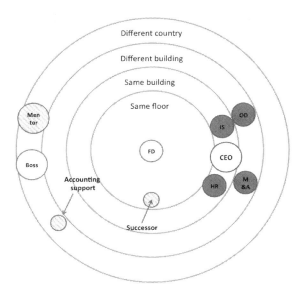

Adding rings to the figure, as shown in Figure 6, introduces geographic proximity. In the closest ring is the successor who sits near Fred's office on the same floor. Located in the same building, the UK headquarters in Leatherhead, is the UK CEO, and the HR and IS leads. These are shown in the next ring out. The OD and M&A colleagues are based in a building in London, so they are shown in the next ring labelled 'different building' and those based overseas—accounting support in Dublin, the European head in Frankfurt, and the mentor in Chicago—are shown in the outer ring.

Figure 7: Fred's Personal Boardroom map, complete

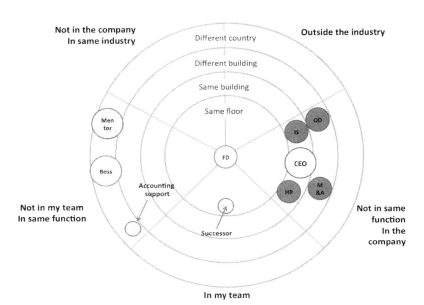

Finally, we add segments to the circles to show where people are drawn from, as in Figure 7. The successor is in Fred's team, so he is shown in bottom segment of the circle. On the left hand lower segment, labelled 'Not in my team, In same Function' are the mentor, boss and the accounting support colleague. These people work within the finance function. On the right-hand side are the others, since these are outside the finance function. There is no one in Fred's Personal Boardroom from outside his company, or outside the industry.

Visualisations like these help to reveal gaps and opportunities. Fred has a good representation of people outside his function, and has two people in other countries who should be able to connect him with developments at the European HQ and in the US. However, he has no one outside his company or industry to keep abreast of innovations in finance, or to introduce fresh perspectives and new ideas. Most of his Boardroom members are people he sees everyday: people who are immersed in the same day-to-day challenges and preoccupations as he is. There is no one to play a 'heads-up' role to help him anticipate the future.

Seeing this map made Fred resolve to connect with the community of finance executives outside the company, and in particular outside his industry, through conferences and dinners. He came to appreciate the value both for his personal reputation in the finance arena, and for the sharing of good practice that he could bring back into his role to benefit the business.

If you like representing information visually, try doing something similar. Once you have drawn your map, look at the distribution, colour and sizes of circles on your map.

- Is there a mix of seniors (large circles) and peers, without being over-dependent on either? Have you included any junior people (small circles)?
- Is there a mix of white, light grey and dark grey showing a breadth that includes both people who are similar in career background, and those who are different? If everyone is very different from you, Chapter 9 tells the story of someone who felt herself to be an outsider, and suggests what to do about it.
- Are you over-dependent on people who work nearby— with a desk near you or in the same building? These are easy people to reach, but could you benefit from making an effort to meet more distant people? Or are you heavily dependent on people overseas? Read in Chapter 9 about what to do if you are an outpost.
- Have you included members of your own team? If not, consider whether your direct reports could be Influencers, Improvers or Challengers for you. Are there senior people (large circles) who are outside your business function? Do you have people outside the company? Outside the industry?

See Chapter 4 for more thoughts on why it is important to include a mix of people across these categories.

## Scoring your Personal Boardroom

Our Personal Boardroom diagnostic tool also includes metrics and charts to quantify the current composition of a Boardroom, and to indicate where it might be improved.

To illustrate this, we use the example of Martha, who we met on a programme for leaders identified as having high potential. We ran a session on the Personal Boardroom for Martha and her colleagues at the beginning of the twelve-month programme.

Martha works in a strategy role in a company's group headquarters. The company was made up of several divisions, and the job of the central strategy unit was to advise the CEO on divestment and acquisition strategies. Martha's Personal Boardroom map is shown in Figure 8.

## Figure 8: Martha's Personal Boardroom map, complete

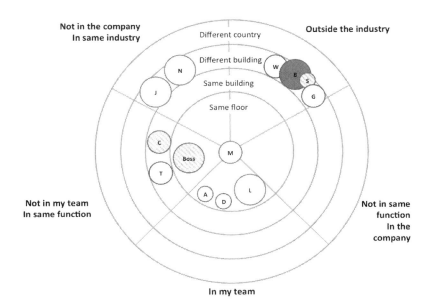

We calculated various metrics to help Martha think about the composition of her Boardroom and identify whether it was where it needed to be. Her scores are shown in the middle column of Table 3. The percentages in Table 3 are calculated by counting the number of roles played by each person in a given category, and expressing this as a proportion of the total number of roles played by everyone in the Boardroom. In Martha's case, there were 12 people in her Boardroom. One person, her boss, played 11 roles of the 12 roles, and on average she had assigned 6 roles to each person. The total role count across all roles played by everyone in Martha's Personal Boardroom was 69.

(To calculate your own total role count, draw a grid with the names of Boardroom members down the left-hand side and the 12 roles across the top. For each role, put the name of each person who plays that role. Your total role count is the total number of ticks on the page.)

Target scores are shown in the right-hand column. These are derived from our knowledge of the research on the network characteristics of high-performers, and our own experience of working with executives.

Table 3: Scores for Martha's Personal Boardroom

| Percentage of roles played by: | Your score | Target score |
|---|---|---|
| Your busiest person | 16% | Less than 25% |
| People inside your company | 58% | Less than 70% |
| People who are located near you | 58% | Less than 50% |
| People with similar or fairly similar career backgrounds to you | 72% | 20% to 40% |
| People who are senior to you | 52% | 30% to 50% |

Martha's boss, the CEO, was a bingo boss, assigned to 11 out of a possible 12 roles. However, he only accounts for 16% of the total role count (as shown in the first data row in Table 3). So although she needs to think carefully about how to structure conversations with her boss to tap into all the value he can bring, she has a coverage of all the roles from others, so her risk of dependency on her boss is not excessive. If a single person accounts for more than 25% of your total role count, you need to take action. (See Chapter 9 for more about bingo bosses.)

*If a single person accounts for more than 25% of your total role count, you are at risk of dependence on that person.*

Martha's map shows that she has a spread of people both within and outside the company, and this is reflected in her score in the second row of Table 3. Colleagues inside the company account for 58% of her total role count. For people in large, complex organisations, we expect Boardroom members to be drawn predominately from inside the company; but if this number creeps over 70%, we think this is too high. The benefits of outside perspectives are lost if a large majority of the focus and the roles are played by people on the inside. In Martha's case, given the internally-focused nature of her role, she recognised the need to invest more time in internal relationships, while also maintaining the strong ties she had with people outside.

You can see from Martha's map in Figure 8 that four of her Boardroom members work on the same floor, and another two in the same building. Beyond these, there is no one else in her company. Colleagues who sit nearby (in the same building, including those on the same floor) account for 58% of her total role count. Martha is over-reliant on people near her.

*No more than 50% of the total role count should come from people who sit near you, because more distant relationships yield novel insights and fresh perspectives.*

A rule of thumb is that no more than 50% of the total role count should come from people who sit near you. This is a particular concern for Martha, as the physical layout of her company is challenging. Each of the business units is located in a different building. We can see from Martha's map that she has no one in any other building, so all of her Boardroom members are either from the group HQ or from outside the company. Since her job is to develop business strategy for the devolved business units, we suggested she needed to build relationships with Navigators, Sponsors and Influencers in each of these units to gain insight into the realities of each business, and to build consensus for the group strategy.

The fourth row of Table 3 illustrates Martha's over-reliance on people who are similar to her in career background. You can see this from the majority of white circles on her map in Figure 8. Throughout this book we have talked about the importance of different perspectives, and this is one of the most valuable aspects of a Personal Boardroom—to learn from people who see things in a different way and can bring fresh ideas and insights. We suggest that no more than 40% of the total role count should be drawn from people who are very similar or fairly similar to you. But we also propose a lower limit, for reasons discussed in Chapter 9, where we described the challenges of seeing yourself as an outsider, and told Nicola's story. Connecting with similar people allows you to benefit from shared vocabulary and frames of reference, and can help to accelerate the effectiveness of a relationship.

*No more than 40% of the total role count should be drawn from people who are similar to you, because of the value of differing perspectives.*

The final row of Table 3 illustrates that Martha is perhaps also slightly over-reliant on people who are senior to her. Of her total role count, 52% comes from people who are senior. You will see from Figure 8 that she has three senior people outside the company, as well as her boss and another senior manager inside. We suggest that no more than 50% of your Boardroom members should be senior to you, because peers and direct reports are so useful as Navigators, Influencers, Challengers and many other roles besides. At the same time, some senior representation is also important (hence the figure of 30% for the bottom of the target range). Even if you are the most senior person in your company, there is still much to be learned from people who have been in your shoes before you, and who are more experienced in your industry.

*No more than 50% of your total role count should be people senior to you, because peers and direct reports are so useful as Navigators, Influencers and Challengers.*

Needless to say, these targets are guidelines, and every person's situation is unique—what we suggest here may not apply to you. But we do find that these metrics lead to useful conversations, which more often than not serve as a prompt to action. Working through these metrics with Martha led to a number of identified actions from her:

- Start to build relationships with people in other business units, initially as Navigators for their businesses, and Challengers for strategy ideas the Group HQ was considering. She recognised the need to invest in these relationships to develop them into Unlockers, Sponsors and Influencers for projects emerging from the central strategy unit.
- Structure her conversations with her boss to benefit from all the different roles he can play for her.
- Be more active about asking peers and direct reports to act as Improvers and Influencers.
- Rebalance how she spends her time, placing a little less emphasis on outside mentors, and freeing up some time to cultivate the internal relationships.

This conversation also led Martha to recognise her own value to her colleagues in other business units. As someone connected into the Group HQ, with oversight of all the business units, she could act as a valuable Navigator and Connector for others on the leadership programme. In the next chapter, we encourage you to think about how you can use the Personal Boardroom roles as a way to structure and drive your contributions to the careers of others.

# Summary of Chapter 10

A strong Personal Boardroom is:

1.  diverse (people from many backgrounds, locations and settings)

2.  balanced (Information, Power and Development roles equally represented)

Visual representations and scores are helpful ways of assessing diversity and balance.

Visualising your Personal Boardroom involves plotting its members on a map to see which categories they are drawn from.

Scoring your Personal Boardroom involves calculating a total role count (a count of roles played by all members) and looking at what percentage of this count is provided by people in a given category.

# 11 Offer help to others

*Be an initiator of generosity.*

Holly Million, film maker[44]

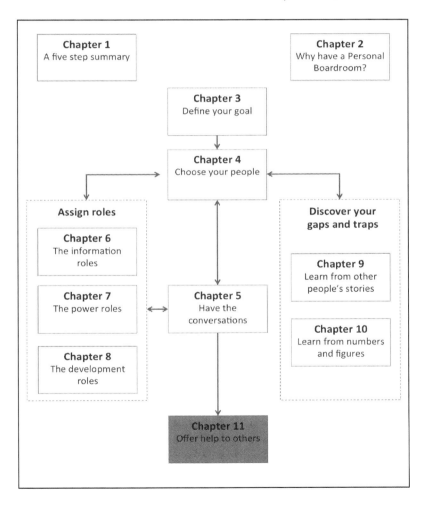

The book so far has been about choosing people for your Personal Boardroom, assigning roles and having conversations with purpose. In this final chapter, we move to the flipside of the Personal Boardroom framework: offering help to others. Although this is the last chapter of the book, it underpins everything that has gone before. Offering help to others is something you do *alongside* your own journey to the Personal Boardroom you need; it is *not* an afterthought.

We start with three principles about paying it forward: being an initiator of generosity; decoupling giving and taking; and putting boundaries around the help you offer. We discuss what's implicit when you offer help to others. We show how to use the 12 Personal Boardroom roles as a structure for offering help. Examples from our own experience of other people generously helping us, or giving help ourselves, are offered in the hope that they might trigger an idea for you.

## The principles of paying it forward

Robert Cialdini, in his classic book *Influence,* states that people say yes to those they owe.[45] People will help you if they owe you for something you did in the past to advance *their* goals. That is the rule of reciprocity.[46] Essentially he is saying that if you put credits in the bank with someone, you'll be able to draw down from them later. That may be true, but we like to think of it differently.

### Be an initiator of generosity

When you ask a Personal Boardroom member, or anyone else, for help, it will not always be possible to reciprocate; and you may not always have had the opportunity to do the 'pre-give' that Cialdini advocates, so you will not always be in a position of credit with someone when you want their help. If they are very senior or very successful, you might also wonder what you could do for them anyway.

*It should not matter if you cannot reciprocate to a Personal Boardroom member, because there will always be someone else you can help.*

In our view, however, that should not matter, because there will always be someone else you can help. If you pay it forward by helping someone else, your contribution will nurture a bigger community of people. That bigger community might be the next generation of leaders in your business, a networking group you belong to, or a group of unemployed young people. The networking organisation BNI is an example of paying it forward in action. Its members, organised into local groups, actively market each other's businesses on the understanding that their own business will benefit from the endorsements of other group members.

It is this network effect that lies at the heart of giving and receiving help in a professional capacity. Vanessa Vallely, entrepreneur and champion of women's careers, talks about this as 'network karma'.[47] You give what you can to people who can use your help, and you feel free to ask for what you need from people who can help you. As we explain further below, the 12 Personal Boardroom roles provide a structure in which you can think about how to give help to others, as well as seeking it for yourself.

For this reason, we prefer Holly Million's words at the beginning of this chapter to those of Robert Cialdini. Be an initiator of generosity. Look for opportunities to do things for other people that will help them along in their careers, without calculating whether that person will be able to do anything for you. Do this, rather, in the expectation that someone else will help you when you ask.

## Decouple giving and taking

According to Adam Grant, Professor at Wharton, most of us in our professional lives are what he calls matchers. Matchers operate on the basis of fairness, and are primarily concerned with maintaining a balance between giving and taking. Matchers don't like to ask favours of people whom they owe, and they are reluctant to give to people who don't reciprocate (takers). At home and with family, our giver tendencies come to the fore. We give to those we love without thinking what they have done for us.[48]

We would like to encourage you to relax the urge to approach every interaction with a matcher's mindset. At the beginning of your Personal Boardroom journey, you're going to feel like a taker. You will be thinking about the value others can bring you, and doing a lot of asking. That is vital, because if you are going to be able to connect from a place of strength as everything changes around you, you have to start by reinforcing your sense of purpose, extending your capabilities, fuelling your power to innovate and to get things done. Your Personal Boardroom will provide that centring force. To build that place of strength, you will need to do some asking. So it's quite possible that the members of your Personal Boardroom will be doing a lot of giving to you.

*Your Personal Boardroom provides the resources that enable you to connect with others from a place of strength.*

We want you to feel comfortable about being a taker in your Personal Boardroom relationships, if that is necessary. Of course, if there is something tangible you can do to help a Boardroom member in return, then you will want do it. Bear in mind also that, for some people, the simple fact of being able to help you will bring them pleasure. (That is likely to apply to Personal Boardroom members who are givers.) But in some cases it may not be possible to do anything very specific to pay a person back.

Feel comfortable about making requests of others, so long as you are also acting as a giver for someone else. That someone else might be a person your Boardroom member cares about. Or your giving may be done outside of any Boardroom relationships. The point is, you try to adopt a giver mindset for some of the time, looking for opportunities to help others. Nourished by the information, power, and development resources that your Personal Boardroom provides, you reach out to share what you can with others.

*Feel comfortable about make requests of others, so long as you are also acting as a giver for someone else.*

What this means is that you make offers of help, as well as responding when people ask. We talk more about this below.

## Put boundaries around your giving

'That's all very well', you might say, 'but how much giving should I do? Isn't there a danger of giving too much? If I spend all my time helping others, won't my productivity suffer?'

The answer is yes and no. Adam Grant's summary of the research on giving and taking shows that being a giver who enjoys helping others can have adverse consequences. In the short term, givers in a sales organisation started out with lower sales revenue, putting their customers' needs before their own sales targets. However, these effects were only evident in the short term. After a year in sales, the highest revenues were brought in by the same generous sales people. Similar findings were observed for generous medical students who had lower grades after one year; by the end of medical school, these students with the most passion for helping others were the highest performers.

So in the short term, it's possible that your productivity will suffer. But in the longer-term Grant says the success of givers comes from two forces: relationships and motivation.[49] Givers build deeper, more trust-based connections, making it more likely that their relationships bring benefits in the long term.

From a motivation perspective, helping others enriches meaning and purpose, energising us to work harder and weather the difficult times. Knowing that their colleagues and patients depended on them, generous medical students were better able to cope with long hours and setbacks.

Although it has long-term performance benefits, giving needs boundaries nonetheless. There is a danger that generosity in the workplace is taken for granted, and this is especially the case for females. A series of studies have shown that volunteering to help colleagues boosted performance evaluations and rewards for men, but not for women.[50]

Successful givers are able to build reputation benefits from their giving. Adam Grant tells the story of Adam Rifkin, an introspective software engineer who built a huge and influential network that included the founders of Facebook, Netscape, Napster, Twitter and Flickr.[51] Rifkin did so by acting as a giver, seeking to contribute to online communities and to help aspiring entrepreneurs in many walks of life. But what is most interesting about Rifkin is that he chose to specialise as a giver. He hated commenting on people's business plans, but he loved bringing people together. So he became a specialist Connector, aiming to make at least three introductions each day.

*Becoming a specialist giver allows you to put boundaries around your giving.*

The genius in Rifkin's strategy is that it places boundaries around his giving. He can satisfy his need for giving, and sustain his reputation, without this being a huge drain on his time. The Personal Boardroom roles provide a mechanism for thinking about specialist giving. If you see yourself as an Expert, you can look for opportunities to offer your expertise to others. If you pride yourself on being able to structure arguments very well, you can specialise as a Challenger. That does not mean you say yes to every request or jump at every opportunity to help; but it does mean you channel your giving in a way that suits you, and brings satisfaction

Even more importantly, becoming a specialist giver allows you to say no. Rifkin says no to business plan requests, and yes to introductions. Some people feel bad or awkward about saying no. You can create boundaries around your giving by being clear (with yourself) about what you are prepared to do for others, and what you are able to do efficiently without a major dent in your productivity.

## How to start a conversation offering help

The vocabulary of the 12 roles is a useful way to initiate an offer for help. As we saw above, you might recognise in yourself a particular strength in one of the roles, and look for opportunities to provide that kind of help to others. Your offer might go something like this:

I know that you are ...

[Mention whatever it is about the person's job, or an immediate challenge that means they might value your help: *e.g.* new to the organisation, trying to raise investment, up for promotion next time round, looking to find a new CFO, *etc.*]

I was just wondering whether there is anything I can do to help you with that. Could you benefit from some help with ...

[Describe the role you have in mind to play: *e.g.* understanding the sector (when offering to be a Navigator); structuring your pitch or business plan (when offering to be a Challenger); giving feedback on their speaking style (when offering to be an Improver).]

As you may know, I ...

[Mention something about what qualifies you for this role.]

I would be very happy to ...

[Explain exactly what you are willing to do, and put clear boundaries around it—how much time, when, *etc.*]

I know you have other people who can help with this, and that sometimes less is more when it comes to advice; so I won't be offended or surprised if you choose not to follow up. Just know that my offer is there if you need it.

In the spirit of paying it forward you might make an offer to one of your Personal Boardroom members, or to someone else, in which you ask if there is anyone they know you could help. For example, if you are offering yourself as an Expert, you could ask if there is someone they know who could use your expertise.

To make a how-can-I-help-someone-you-know offer, your approach might be something like this:

I'm very grateful for the way you have been able to help me with ...

[Mention whatever the person has done for you and why it has been, or will be, so important and useful to you.]

As a way of saying thank you for your invaluable support, I wonder if there is someone you know who I could help. As you know I have a lot of experience with/insight into/a knack for/connections with ...

[With your chosen role in mind, describe what it is that you are offering: *e.g.* understanding the sector (when offering to be a Navigator); structuring your pitch or business plan (when offering to be a Challenger); giving feedback on their speaking style (when offering to be an Improver).]

> If one or two people you know could benefit from that, I would be very happy to ...
>
> [Explain exactly what you are willing to do and put clear boundaries around it—how much time, how many people, what type of person, *etc.*]

## What's implicit in the offer?

Much of your giving may be in response to requests, but we want to encourage unprompted offers of help too. The first part of this chapter suggested you offer help without necessarily expecting anything in return. That means your offer might be unprompted: you will be taking the initiative to suggest how you could help someone.

You will recall from the chapters on the 12 Personal Boardroom roles that we discussed what is implicit in the ask for each role. In the same way, when you offer help, some things are not always made explicit.

When we help someone by giving advice, there can be an expectation that they will embrace our wisdom and act on it. Especially where an offer is unprompted, you might be driven by a strong sense that you are doing the 'right thing'. Not everyone sees things the same way you do. So in your approach, try to offer humbly and let your intended recipient know that they can opt out without causing offence. If you do expect something in return, however, it is much better to say so than to leave your recipient guessing.

When making unprompted offers of help, try to see it as an invitation, not an obligation. Avoiding a sense of obligation in your recipient can be difficult, but it is possible if you are careful to explain your motivation. Think about your reasons for giving. Are you motivated to give because of **who** the person is; the **challenge** they face; or because you believe in the **cause,** or an outcome that will result from what they are doing? (See the beginning of Chapter 5 for more on these motivations.)

*When making unprompted offers of help, try to make it feel like an invitation, not an obligation.*

Always be aware that, when you make an offer of help, you are not asking to be a member of someone else's Personal Boardroom. You cannot make that decision for someone else. As we saw in Chapter 5, people may choose to keep who is in their Personal Boardroom private. So while the vocabulary of the twelve roles is a very effective way to initiate an offer for help, avoid making it sound like you are asking to be a member of someone's Personal Boardroom.

## Offering help: the Personal Boardroom roles

In this section we hope to trigger some ideas about how you might offer help to others, using the Personal Boardroom roles as a guide. We look at each role in turn, with an illustrative story and a few questions to ask yourself. The stories we provide below are from our own experience either in offering or receiving help. We have included some examples of unprompted offers, and some examples where the giver went considerably beyond an initial request for help. Unlike the rest of the book, names in this chapter have not been changed.

### Offering help as a Customer Voice

 When you offer help as a Customer Voice, you are speaking to someone as their customer, or as a potential customer. You point out aspects of their service or product that they may not be aware of.

You describe the strengths and weaknesses of a competitor's product. You help them understand a market they are trying to sell to.

Although we use the word customer, we also include investors, employees or service-users. As an investor, you might be able to help someone understand what they need to do to make their proposition investable; and as an employee you could make observations about how your colleagues feel about their workplace, or the actions of senior managers. Do so in the spirit of making the proposition or the workplace better.

*When you offer help as a Customer Voice, you are speaking to someone as their customer, or as a potential customer.*

Maria O'Donoghue, vice president, global learning and talent management at Hertz has been a very important Customer Voice for us. Amanda's initial request was for Maria's feedback. We wanted her views on our idea for using the Personal Boardroom framework as a tool for accelerated transition coaching for executives. Maria embraced what we were doing and (acting as an Unlocker) invited us to work with some Hertz managers and executives who were making internal moves. Since then, as a Customer Voice, she has made suggestions about how our offering could be tailored for inclusion in leadership-development programmes for female leaders, and gone to some lengths to show us what existing providers are offering in that space.

Amanda did a business development course run by Joanne Hession of QED. Joanne didn't deliver the programme herself. Amanda had some questions about the selection and recruitment of the participants on the course, and thought that Joanne might find her feedback useful. They arranged to meet for coffee, and Amanda offered a list of suggestions about what worked well and what could be improved. As a business owner,

Joanne was appreciative of the feedback because she had not been present to observe the course herself.

Ask yourself:

- Who do you buy from, as an individual or as a business?
- What could you tell them about their own product or service, or about the competition, that could help them deliver better for the customer?
- Can you be an employee voice to help make your workplace a better place to work?
- Can you pass on insights as an investor to help someone make their business more attractive to invest in?

## Offering help as an Expert

 When you offer help as an Expert, you are inviting people to make use of your expertise for free. A common example is the *pro bono* work that professionals, such as lawyers and accountants, do for clients or charities who could not afford their services.

There is a fine line to tread if you make a living from the kind of advice you are offering. Try to make it clear what you are able to do for free, and why. If you are genuinely not expecting any business in return, explain your motivation for helping, and release the recipient from a feeling of obligation to you.

*When you offer help as an Expert, you are inviting people to make use of your expertise.*

Zella was looking for advice on protecting the personal data of our clients. She searched online and found David Taylor, a consultant in the area. She picked up the phone. David answered immediately and in the course of a 45-minute conversation, gave her an extensive briefing, including some detail on the UK's Information Commissioner's Office, and how to handle the transfer of personal data outside the EU. Because our business is a start-up, David also sent templates of legal documents that he would normally charge for. He was very clear that Zella owed nothing in return (although she did promise to send David a copy of this book!).

Five years ago, Amanda ran a network for female entrepreneurs in the West of Ireland. One of its members, Cristina Luminea, worked in the area of social media. Cristina offered to help Amanda set up social networking platforms so that the group, which had previously only connected face to face, could interact online. This was something Amanda had been struggling with, so Cristina's expertise was very welcome. Cristina did not ask to be paid for her time because she saw herself as creating value for the network as a whole.

Ask yourself:

* Who could benefit from your expertise?
* Is there a shareable, non-competitive nugget—perhaps about some new development in your professional domain—which someone would benefit from knowing?

## Offering help as an Inspirer

When you offer help as an Inspirer, you are passing on delightful discoveries and exciting content to someone else. Discovery is a serendipitous process—often we don't know what we need to know until we stumble on it—so by sharing you are putting something out there that night nudge someone to a new insight, or open up a new vista. You cannot know what someone else will make of your ideas. As an Inspirer you simply offer it and let go.

*When you offer help as an Inspirer, you are passing on delightful discoveries and exciting content to someone else.*

One of our most prolific Inspirers, Andy Burnett, describes his job as helping smart people have creative conversations about important problems. The work involves bringing academics and scientists of different disciplines together to create ground-breaking research ideas. Every day, around a thousand science blog feeds come into Andy's inbox. He scans them, picks out a few that are exciting, interesting, or just funny. He forwards these to a couple of people who might find them relevant. Andy has inspired us, and no doubt hundreds of others, with his stream of unprompted, thought-provoking insights.

Ask yourself:

- What discoveries have you stumbled across in the press, in a book, on YouTube, or in a trade journal, that excited you? Who might enjoy hearing about them?
- Who are your weak ties—people who move in different worlds? Research shows that innovation often results where people have the opportunity to combine insights from different fields or specialisms. Could you help a weak tie to be innovative by sharing something that's going on in your world?

## Offering help as a Navigator

 When you offer help as a Navigator, you are giving someone else an overview of a world that you know better than they do. That might be talking about the most dominant suppliers in a particular area, and who runs them. It might be explaining who makes purchasing decisions, or how the budgeting or performance-calibration processes work. You might let a senior manager know how a change she initiated is perceived by people lower down in the organisation, and where resistance lies.

*When you offer help as a Navigator, you are giving someone else an overview of a world that you know better than they do.*

Amanda met Chaw Kalayar on a 'back-to-work' programme, and was impressed by her determination. Chaw had put herself through college, graduating with a first-class degree in Pharmaceutical Science. Having left Burma with her young family, she had no network to help her tap into Ireland's job market, in which connections are often the best way to find out about jobs. Amanda wanted to help, so she put together a list of all the HR heads in the region. She had to send a few emails to people in her network to get an up-to-date list. Amanda gave Chaw a list of 15 people, and helped her write a speculative letter to each.

Ask yourself:

- How do promotions work in your part of the business? What is the selection process really like for external hires? How are budget decisions made? Who calls the shots in purchasing decisions? These questions are easy to answer when you have been in a company for a while. But for newcomers and junior colleagues, it can be hard to tell.
- Who could benefit from hearing about an industry or a professional community you know well?

## Offering help as an Unlocker

 When you offer help as a Unlocker, you make resources available to someone who would not otherwise be able to access them. The resources could be money, people's time, systems, data, equipment, desk space, meeting rooms, or other facilities.

Offering help as an Unlocker is likely to be very enabling. Be aware that your offer may well trigger in the recipient a strong sense of obligation or indebtedness. If you do expect something in return it is better to say so. Avoiding that sense of obligation can be difficult, but it is possible if you are careful to explain your motivation.

> *When you offer help as a Unlocker, you make resources available to someone who would not otherwise be able to access them.*

A few years ago, Amanda started a business coaching women returning to work after maternity leave. Her neighbour, Nadine Nohr, was interested in coaching and liked the approach Amanda was taking. Nadine ran a large sales team at Granada, and offered Amanda the opportunity to work with two women as 'guinea pigs' for her new service. The resource she unlocked for Amanda was time with her people, which enabled Amanda to gain very valuable experience of working with clients.

Ask yourself:

- What do you control that others struggle to get hold of? Think about money, but also people's time, systems, data, equipment, venues, facilities, *etc.*
- Who could benefit if you were to open up access, or make an offer to share?
- Can you be very clear about your motivation for making your offer, and anything you expect in return?

## Offering help as a Sponsor

 When offering help as a Sponsor, you are stating your willingness to speak out on someone's behalf about them, or their product or company. That might be by writing a reference, supporting their promotion or acting as a reference client. LinkedIn now makes this very easy to do in an unprompted way through its recommendations, which are publicly visible. Online endorsements are useful, but offline much more so, and are especially powerful when offered by a client or former client.

*When you offer help as a Sponsor, you are willing to speak out about someone, or their product or company.*

We were fortunate to meet Liam Black, of The Same Wavelength, at a speaking event. We were not *bona fide* invitees at the event—we were both there at someone else's request. Liam not only agreed to our tagging along, but proceeded to invite Zella to lunch to learn more about our business. He and his colleague Adrian Simpson have become great Sponsors of our work, talking about it to their clients, and creating opportunities for us to showcase what we do at their events.

Acts of sponsorship can, of course, be unprompted. Amanda remembers William Eccleshare, now CEO of Clear Channel Outdoor Holdings, from her early years at J Walter Thompson. William played the role of Sponsor as if he had written the script himself. He spotted her during the recruitment process and put her on his team running the Kellogg's account. He argued hard for pay rises and bonuses, and when another graduate asked to be given a company car, he insisted that there was one for Amanda too. It was only when he changed role that Amanda realised how much of his support she had taken for granted.

Ask yourself:

- Whose work do you respect highly? Think about your team, but also about people elsewhere in your business, and about suppliers and partners.
- If you were to write an endorsement, or publicly state your appreciation, would that make a real difference to them?
- Sponsorship by clients or former clients is especially powerful. Can you help one of your suppliers by providing a client endorsement?

## Offering help as an Influencer

 When offering help as an Influencer, you are expressing your willingness to have a private conversation that will push a project along, or open up an opportunity for someone. This is an unusual role in that the work of Influencer is often invisible to the person who benefits.

*When you offer help as an Influencer, you are willing to have a private conversation that will advance a project or open up an opportunity.*

On several occasions, we have been able to secure business thanks to the quiet support of people who first made an introduction to their colleagues in Learning and Development, and then appeared to step out of the way. We do not know what conversations were had behind the scenes, but we strongly suspect that our initial Connectors were also Influencers.

Amanda was approached by a friend, Patricia, a retired doctor, who wanted to set up an information website that would help women considering breast cancer screening. Her friend, not a technical whizzkid, was putting off the decision to get someone to build the website, because she'd been given some hefty quotes and she didn't know what she should pay. She and Amanda had a mutual friend in Susan, a digital marketeer. Amanda encouraged Patricia to have another conversation with Susan before looking elsewhere. Amanda explained what she liked about Susan's service (the hands-on coaching support to help her clients mobilise inbound traffic to their websites); and how she thought Patricia could use aspects of that.

Ask yourself:

• Do you know someone with a great idea or project who need encouragement, or who is struggling to build support or gather resources?

- Is there a conversation you could have with someone likely to be resistant to their idea: someone who respects you? Could that conversation unlock something for them?

## Offering help as a Connector

 When offering help as a Connector, you are opening up your book of contacts and inviting someone to borrow a little of your social capital. Unprompted emails along the lines of 'you two should meet' are, happily, very common. However, that action is all the more effective if you can explain to each party exactly what you see is valuable, by closing the triangle and putting them in touch. And even more powerful still is the question: 'who can I introduce you to?'

> *When you offer help as a Connector, you are inviting someone to borrow a little of your social capital.*

After years in the Irish banking industry, and running a Chamber of Commerce in Dublin, John McGrane has a huge network in Ireland and elsewhere. On several occasions, we have had dinner with John, and he has asked us who we would like to be introduced to. As a Connector, the particularly impressive thing about John is his intuition for timing. At our first meeting, aware that we did not yet have a clearly articulated proposition, John said, 'I can make the introductions. Just let me know when you're ready.'

A journalist friend of Amanda's called while struggling with an article on sleep, and the impact of lack of sleep on decision-making and productivity at work. Although this isn't Amanda's line of work, she was able to make an introduction to a resilience coach, who in turn was glad of the publicity opportunity.

Ask yourself:

- Where is there real potency in introducing two people you know who have professional interests or personal situations in common?
- Think about your weak ties—people who move in a different social or professional setting to you. By creating a bridge between people who don't know each other, what value could you create for them?
- Have you thought of asking the question 'who could I introduce you to?', rather than making your own assumptions about who would be useful?

## Offering help as an Improver

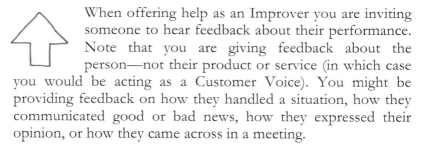 When offering help as an Improver you are inviting someone to hear feedback about their performance. Note that you are giving feedback about the person—not their product or service (in which case you would be acting as a Customer Voice). You might be providing feedback on how they handled a situation, how they communicated good or bad news, how they expressed their opinion, or how they came across in a meeting.

Not all feedback is welcomed, and not everyone is ready to hear it, so bear this in mind when you offer. If you haven't been asked for feedback, broach your offer as a suggestion, and wait for the person to accept. Find a way to provide your feedback when the person is in the right frame of mind to receive it, but ideally as close to the event concerned as possible. If you do not have specific examples to support your feedback, consider whether it is a good idea to offer it.

*When you offer help as an Improver you are inviting someone to hear feedback about their performance.*

Dan Cobley, former MD of Google UK and Ireland, told us about giving feedback to a boss who was based in the US, with a team spread across the US and Europe. Dan noticed that, while his boss claimed to be even-handed in dividing his attention between the US and Europe, the examples he gave on team calls were always about clients and activities in the US. Dan let his boss know that the European members of his team felt isolated by this, and encouraged him to over-play examples from outside the US to create a feeling of inclusion.

Ask yourself:

- Whose performance do you regularly observe—in meetings, speaking from a stage, in e-mail correspondence, on camera? What feedback—both positive and developmental—could you offer?
- Think in particular of people senior to you, who rarely have the opportunity to hear constructive opinions on their performance.
- Do you have specific examples that you can use to support what you are saying?

## Offering help as a Challenger

 When offering help as a Challenger, you are making yourself available to comment on and improve something a person is doing. That might be a document or a presentation they are planning to make. Your comments come *before* the event, not afterwards, and the consequence of your involvement will be that the decision, document, or pitch meeting turns out better.

*When you offer help as a Challenger, you are making yourself available to comment on and improve something.*

While writing this book we sent drafts to a number of people for comments. But the most awe-inspiring response was from someone who said he had only read two books in his life, and one of them was the draft book we sent him. We had a lively debate about reciprocity in relationships and the Cialdini quote discussed at the beginning of this chapter. We did not agree with everything he said, but the conversation was instrumental in shaping the arguments for this chapter.

One PA we know takes it upon herself to ensure that whenever her boss is making a big presentation, she checks what he is wearing. She doesn't spare his blushes and will happily tell him to change his tie, jacket or trousers if she thinks that they aren't suitable for the occasion.

A colleague of Amanda's was approaching an interview for a promotion into a role she was competing with colleagues for. Amanda helped her prepare by providing feedback on her CV, and showing her how to structure her responses to interview questions. After the interview Amanda received an appreciative email: *I'm really happy with how I handled myself, and the pre-work was 100% to thank for that. Thank you so much for your time on my behalf.*

Ask yourself:

- Is there someone whose work frustrates you because you know it could be better? Do you find yourself telling them that after an event, rather than beforehand when they could have done something about it?
- Are there some guidelines you can offer to improve the clarity, persuasiveness or impact of their work? Include people outside your team, and people who would not necessarily think to call on you to challenge their assumptions, but who could benefit if you did.

## Offering help as a Nerve-Giver

 When offering help as a Nerve-Giver you are expressing your desire to help them make a commitment to a course of action, or to continuing on that course. You may also be acknowledging that someone needs a boost of confidence. Perhaps they are facing a tough decision or struggling with the consequences of having made one. People do not always find such situations easy to acknowledge. Look for signs that you have read the situation correctly.

*When you offer help as a Nerve-Giver you are expressing your desire to help someone make a commitment to a course of action, or to continuing on that course.*

A client told Amanda about an unprompted Nerve-Giver moment. The client, who we'll call Alison, was walking along the corridor feeling very distressed. She had just walked out of a very difficult meeting with a new CEO. The HR director stopped her in the corridor and asked what was up. Alison explained that she felt the new CEO had walked all over her. The HR director reminded her of all that she had done to get to her very senior position, and that she needed to honour that investment. He looked at her squarely and told her to go back into the meeting and 'finish the job' she had worked so hard for.

Ask yourself:

- Who has recently made a tough decision that you respect?
- Who do you know who is facing a difficult situation?
- Is there anything you can do to support them, and reinforce their conviction that their decision and the subsequent actions were the right things to do?

## Offering help as an Anchor

 When offering help as an Anchor you are expressing an interest or a concern about someone's work-life balance. You are asking for permission to touch on aspects of their life that might be quite private or sensitive, such as a loss of motivation, a relationship breakdown, or a lifestyle issue. Make sure the person is ready and willing to talk about the wider context of their life, not just the persona they portray at work. Some organisations encourage this, by making work-life balance, and employees' ratings of that, a priority for their managers. But in a culture where this is not encouraged, make the offer carefully.

*When you offer help as an Anchor you are asking for permission to talk about something that could be private or sensitive.*

Dan Cobley told us how, as MD of Google UK, he tried to act as an Anchor for his direct reports. His team were highly driven and competitive sales executives, who worked long hours and often spent evenings entertaining clients. Dan made a point of finding out what they liked to do outside work to ensure they made time for what was most important. One of his team was a very keen tennis player. So Dan made a point of asking, at every one-on-one meeting, when he had last played. Tennis joined the list of deliverables that were reported on each week. This was Dan's way of making sure his team member made time for tennis. And by doing something similar for each team member, Dan hoped to keep them anchored in what was important to them outside work.

Ask yourself:

- Are there subtle (or not so subtle) ways you can nudge your team or colleagues to take care of their lives outside work?
- Do you know someone who seems to have lost motivation and energy? Can you remind them why their work is important?
- Is there anyone in your team, or someone close to you, who seems anxious, excessively tired, struggling with their weight, or out of control? Is there a discreet, respectful way to express your concern about their well-being?

## Conclusion

The legendary Stephen Covey says that highly effective people are able to make a transition from being dependent on others for learning, to being independent.[52] Independent people take responsibility for choices and the consequences that follow—in work and in life.

But beyond independent, effective people are *inter*dependent: they value and respect others, listen well, are open-minded enough to be influenced by others, and create mutually beneficial and supportive relationships.

Our hope is that this book will help you on a journey towards interdependence. We hope it will show you how to build and benefit from a Personal Boardroom that sustains and inspires you, and gives you the power to sustain and inspire others.

# Summary of Chapter 11

---

The three principles of paying it forward:

1. Be an initiator of generosity.

2. Decouple giving and taking, so that you don't worry about the balance of reciprocity in individual relationships.

3. Put boundaries around your giving.

When making unprompted offers of help, try to make it feel like an invitation, not an obligation.

Use the twelve Personal Boardroom roles as a way to organise the help you give.

---

## What to do now

Let us know what you think of this book. It is a work in progress. We would love to hear your stories of how the book helped you, or someone you know, and how we can improve it. Feel free to contact us at admin@personalboardroom.com.

If you would like to know more about what we do, or if you are interested in licensing and using the Personal Boardroom diagnostic tool in your own work as a coach or trainer, please visit our website at www.personalboardroom.com.

Zella, left, is an Executive Fellow at Henley Business School. She began her career as a consultant (Accenture) and an investment banker (Schroders). She earned her PhD in Occupation Psychology from Birkbeck College, London. Over a 12-year career as an academic her articles on careers and organisational networks have appeared in top management and business journals.

Amanda, right, spent six years as an advertising executive with J. Walter Thompson before becoming an agent for actors and directors. Returning to her roots in psychology and her interest in change, she is now an executive coach based in Ireland.

In 2012 we started looking for ways to apply research evidence about the networks of high-performers to the real world. Our collaboration led us to the idea of a Personal Boardroom as a way to help people think purposefully about the network they need in order to succeed. The concept has proved to be intuitive, simple to apply, and popular with executives in coaching and classroom settings. This book is the product of that work.

# Acknowledgements

Many people have been generous in helping us develop the ideas in this book. Here we mention just a few of them, and the roles they have played for us. This list is far from complete; we have been helped in numerous ways by others. Thank you to everyone who is accompanying us on our journey.

**Customer Voices**: Charles Mindenhall, Niall O'Reilly, Teresa Purtill, Mark Onyett, Mark Sanders

**Experts**: Anthony Basker, Adrian King, Jeremy Gardner, Ian Gotts, Stephen Parker, Janet Sheath, David Taylor

**Inspirers**: Andy Burnett, Adrian Keogh, Paul King, Ingrid Wassenaar

**Navigators**: Charlotte Balbirnie, Steven Beard, Matt Clifford, Gary Flynn, Birgit Neu, Phil Rose

**Unlockers**: Oonagh Monahan, Maria O'Donoghue, Rob Sumroy, Claire Whittingham

**Sponsors**: Manoj Badale, Andy Baker, Liam Black, Matt Brittin, Ginny Gibson, Julia Hobsbawm

**Influencers**: Francis Lake, Toby McHenry, Jill Miller, Parm Sandhu, Mark Smith

**Connectors**: John McGrane, Rowena Neville, Andrew Parish, Adrian Simpson, Isobel Tynan

**Improvers**: Rhonda Doyle, James Elias, Laura Gordon, Caroline Hickson, Tariq Janmohamed, Emilia Stubbs

**Challengers**: Doug Kalish, Karen Lord, Cristina Luminea, Geoff McDonald, Janet Walsh, Greville Ward

**Nerve-Givers**: Scott Cain, Clive Garland, Elisabeth Hobbs, Joe King, Phil Williams

**Anchors**: Lavinia Greacen, Sheila Jones, Sue King

And of course, thank you to our 'bingo spouses', Toby and Dan, and to our gorgeous and tolerant children, Callum, Robyn, Hadley, Tom and Ben.

Amanda remembers Walter Greacen, a great Connector, with love.

# References

1 Peter Sims is co-author of a book called *True North: Discovering your Authentic Leadership*, written with Harvard academic Bill George. This quote comes from a Huffington Post article, featuring an interview with Bill George about his new book, *True North Groups: A Powerful Path to Personal and Leadership Development*. Article accessed 8 October 2014. http://www.huffingtonpost.com/peter-sims/youre-only-as-good-as-who_b_956565.html

2 See Jim Collins' article 'Looking out for number one' accessed 8 October 2014 http://www.jimcollins.com/article_topics/articles/looking-out.html

3 See http://leanin.org/circles for more about the Lean In group movement set up by Sheryl Sandberg to encourage women to pursue their career ambitions.

4 The Young Presidents' Organization promotes Forum Groups in which young chief executives support each other. See http://www.ypo.org

5 True North Groups are intimate groups in which people from any background join together, often on a long-standing basis, to discuss both personal and professional matters and life's important questions. The movement emphasises fulfillment, reaching potential and self-awareness. See http://www.truenorthgroups.com/

6 Mastermind groups encourage brainstorming with others, creating goals, holding each other accountable, and

encouraging a positive mental attitude. See
http://www.thesuccessalliance.com/

7  Rob Cross, at the University of Virginia, and Jonathon
   Cummings at MIT showed that in knowledge-intensive work,
   certain network properties increase the quality and relevance
   of the information people receive, and thereby improve their
   performance. This included having links with people outside
   their department or business unit, with people that span
   physical boundaries (for example to other locations) and with
   people senior in the hierarchy. Data from 101 engineers in a
   petrochemical company and 125 consultants in a strategy-
   consulting firm showed that people with these network
   characteristics had higher levels of performance. Appraisal
   data, peer feedback and objective data on project outcomes
   were used to measure performance. These findings are
   reported in Cross R. and Cummings J.N., Tie and network
   correlates of individual performance in knowledge-intensive
   work, *Academy of Management Journal*, 2004, 47(6): 926-937. In
   another study at an investment bank (reported in Cross, R.
   and Thomas, R.J., 2009, *Driving Results through Social Networks:
   How Top Organizations leverage networks for Performance and
   Growth*, Jossey-Bass), Cross showed that newly promoted
   senior vice presidents were more likely then their non-
   promoted peers to have bridging networks that connected
   them with people in different business units, with different
   expertise and in different tenure groupings: *i.e.* people who
   had spent either more or less time at the bank. A Harvard
   Business Review paper (Cross, R., and Thomas, R. 2011, A
   Smarter Way to Network, *Harvard Business Review*, July-
   August) summarises some of Rob Cross's research findings
   drawn from his work with over 100 organisations.

8  Monica Higgins and David Thomas studied the relationship
   constellations of lawyers in corporate law firms. Higgins and
   Thomas made a distinction between a primary developer—a

boss, mentor or sponsor—and their entire constellation of developmental relationships. The quality of a person's relationship with their primary developer explained short-term outcomes like work satisfaction, but it was the composition and quality of the entire constellation of relationships that accounted for long-term outcomes such as promotion to partner. This research is reported in Higgins, M. and Thomas D., 2001, Constellations and careers: toward understanding the effects of multiple developmental relationships, *Journal of Organizational Behavior*, 22(3): 223-247.

9 In an earlier draft of the book we had a chapter drawing out a number of insights from this body of academic research. If you are interested in knowing more about the research foundations on which this book is based, please contact us at admin@personalboardroom.com.

10 If you haven't yet had the chance to complete the diagnostic, you can find some of the questions it asks in Chapter 10. For more details about how to access a report, visit our website at www.personalboardroom.com.

11 Robert Cialdini, 2007, *Influence: The Psychology of Persuasion*, Harper Business; Revised Edition.

12 In a TED Radio Hour episode on Disruptive Leadership, broadcast 17 January 2014, Sheryl Sandberg discussed a TED talk she had previously given on how to cultivate women leaders. As part of the interview she made this quote while referring to the changes organisations can make straight away. We like this quote for its 'get on and do it now!' feel. The Sandberg interview can be found at http://www.npr.org/programs/ted-radio-hour/261084166/disruptive-leadership. Accessed 11 September 2014.

13 Ben Horowitz, 2014, *The Hard Thing about Hard Things: Building a business when there are no easy answers*, Harper Collins, page ix

14 Ben Horowitz describes his experience as co-founder and CEO of Opsware, formerly Loudcloud, which was ultimately acquired by Hewlett Packard for $1.6 billion 2007, in his book, *The Hard Thing about Hard Things: Building a business when there are no easy answers*, published by Harper Collins

15 All of the examples on pages 27 to 29 are taken from Ben Horowitz's book, *The Hard Thing about Hard Things: Building a business when there are no easy answers*, published by Harper Collins. The quote about Andreessen is on pp 14-15.

16 Simon Sinek, 2011, *Start With Why: How Great Leaders Inspire Everyone To Take Action*, Penguin

17 Ben Horowitz, 2014, *The Hard Thing about Hard Things: Building a business when there are no easy answers*, Harper Collins, p 37

18 Lisa Gansky shared this at an event organised for The Same Wavelength's Connect programme in March 2014. See http://thesamewavelength.com/connect

19 Nikos Mourkogiannis, 2006, *Purpose, The Starting Point of Great Companies*, Palgrave Macmillan

20 *This mission statement can be found on numerous Unilever websites around the world, including this one:* http://www.unileverme.com/aboutus/ourvision/ Accessed 11 September 2014 .

21 The concept of a circle of influence comes from Steven Covey's *The Seven Habits of Highly Effective People*, which has

been published in numerous editions including a 2004 edition by Simon & Schuster Ltd.

22 Marcus Buckingham's book *StandOut*, published 2011, by Thomas Nelson Publishers, explores what makes us at our most powerful, as perceived by others.

23 Quoted on http://www.brainyquote.com/quotes/authors/s/stephen_c how.html Accessed 11 September 2014

24 Thanks to Andy Burnett, Inspirer, who originated this way of thinking divergently about who you need in your network.

25 The strength of weak ties theory, advanced by Mark Granovetter in the 1970s, argued that so-called weak ties are more useful than strong ties for finding a job. Within any social clique, ties are likely to be strong—*i.e.* intense, frequent and overlapping, meaning that people in the group have a lot of connections in common. These strong ties within social groups mean that information is generally shared quickly, and most people know the same things. Ties with people outside your social group, on the other hand, are more likely to generate new information, such as news about job openings. Such relationships are more likely to be infrequent and held at arm's length. Granovetter referred to these as weak ties. A second edition of the book in which he set out these ideas, *Getting a Job: Study of Contacts and Careers*, was published by University of Chicago Press in 1995. The benefits of a network structure that spans social worlds for creativity was shown by Ron Burt in his 2004 paper Structural Holes and Good Ideas, *American Journal of Sociology*, 110(2), 161-177.

26 Adam Grant introduced us to the term 'dormant relationships' in his book *Give and Take: Why helping others drives our success*, 2013, Phoenix.

27 Rob Cross and Andrew Parker talk about energising and de-energising behaviour in their 2004 book, *The Hidden Power of Social Networks: Understanding How Work Really Gets Done in Organizations*, Harvard Business School Press.

28 Quoted in *Brewers' Dictionary of Phrase and Fable*, 1995, Orion Publishing

29 Adam Grant, 2013, *Give and Take: Why helping others drives our success*, Phoenix.

30 Adam Grant's online resources can be found at www.giveandtake.com

31 Various TED talks by Julian Treasure can be found at http://www.ted.com/speakers/julian_treasure

32 Quoted in *Brewers' Dictionary of Phrase and Fable*, 1995, Orion Publishing

33 Ben Horowitz, 2014, *The Hard Thing about Hard Things: Building a business when there are no easy answers*, Harper Collins, p 36

34 Quoted on Wikiquote, http://en.wikiquote.org/wiki/Alice_Walker Accessed 22 September 2014

35 Ben Horowitz, 2014, *The Hard Thing about Hard Things: Building a business when there are no easy answers*, Harper Collins, p 44

36 John and Carol's story is told in Julie Battilana and Tiziana Casciaro's 2013 paper The Network Secrets of Great Change Agents, *Harvard Business Review*, July-August: 2-8.

37 Quoted in *Brewers' Dictionary of Phrase and Fable*, 1995, Orion Publishing

38 Ben Horowitz, 2014, *The Hard Thing about Hard Things: Building a business when there are no easy answers*, Harper Collins, p 23

39 *op cit* p. 8

40 John Kotter, Forbes magazine, 12 April 2006 http://www.forbes.com/2006/04/12/power-of-stories-oped-cx_jk_0412kotter.html Accessed 11 September 2014

41 Interview with Valdis Krebs http://thrivable.net/2010/11/network-thinking-interview-with-valdis-krebs/ Accessed 11 September 2014

42 Quoted on http://www.analyticshero.com/2012/10/25/31-essential-quotes-on-analytics-and-data/ Accessed 11 September 2014

43 For more on Lean In groups, see www.leanin.org

44 We are indebted to Holly Million who made this insightful comment to Zella when they met in October 2012.

45 Robert Cialdini, 2007, *Influence: The Psychology of Persuasion*, Harper Business; Revised Edition.

46 Cialdini interview in *Harvard Business Review* http://hbr.org/2013/07/the-uses-and-abuses-of-influence/ar/1

47 Private conversation with Vanessa Vallely, founder of WeAreTheCity.com May 2014

48 Adam Grant says that givers tend to pay attention to what other people need from them. They may give without any expectation of a return, and if they do a cost-benefit analysis, it is only to consider whether the benefit to others exceeds the personal cost to them. Adam Grant, 2013, *Give and Take: Why helping others drives our success*, Phoenix

49 See Adam Grant's article in *The Atlantic: How to succeed professionally by helping others.* http://www.theatlantic.com/health/archive/2014/03/how-to-succeed-professionally-by-helping-others/284429/

50 *op cit.*

51 Adam Grant, 2013, *Give and Take: Why helping others drives our success*, Phoenix

52 Stephen R. Covey, 2004, *The Seven Habits of Highly Effective People*, Simon & Schuster

20216500R00125

Printed in Great Britain
by Amazon